Cambridge Elements ≡

Elements in Publishing and Book Culture
edited by
Samantha Rayner
University College London
Leah Tether
University of Bristol

PUBLISHING IN WALES

Renaissance and Resistance

Jacob D. Rawlins
Brigham Young University

CAMBRIDGE
UNIVERSITY PRESS

CAMBRIDGE
UNIVERSITY PRESS

University Printing House, Cambridge CB2 8BS, United Kingdom

One Liberty Plaza, 20th Floor, New York, NY 10006, USA

477 Williamstown Road, Port Melbourne, VIC 3207, Australia

314–321, 3rd Floor, Plot 3, Splendor Forum, Jasola District Centre, New Delhi – 110025, India

103 Penang Road, #05–06/07, Visioncrest Commercial, Singapore 238467

Cambridge University Press is part of the University of Cambridge.

It furthers the University's mission by disseminating knowledge in the pursuit of education, learning, and research at the highest international levels of excellence.

www.cambridge.org
Information on this title: www.cambridge.org/9781108948173
DOI: 10.1017/9781108951159

© Jacob D. Rawlins 2022

First published 2022

A catalogue record for this publication is available from the British Library.

ISBN 978-1-108-94817-3 Paperback
ISSN 2514-8524 (online)
ISSN 2514-8516 (print)

Publishing in Wales

Renaissance and Resistance

Elements in Publishing and Book Culture

DOI: 10.1017/9781108951159
First published online: April 2022

Jacob D. Rawlins
Brigham Young University

Author for correspondence: Jacob D. Rawlins, jacob_rawlins@byu.edu

ABSTRACT: The creation of texts preserves culture, literature, myths, and society, and provides invaluable insights into history. Yet we still have much to learn about the history of how those texts were produced and how the production of texts has influenced modern societies, particularly in smaller nations like Wales. The story of publishing in Wales is closely connected to the story of Wales itself. Wales, the Welsh people, and the Welsh language have survived invasion, migration, oppression, revolt, resistance, religious and social upheavals, and economic depression. The books of Wales chronicle this story and the Welsh people's endurance over centuries of challenges. Ancient law books, medieval manuscripts, legends and myths, secretly printed religious works, poetry, song, social commentary, and modern novels tell a story of a tiny nation, its hardy people, and an enduring literary legacy that has an outsized influence on culture and literature far beyond the Welsh borders.

This Element also has a video abstract: www.cambridge.org/rawlins

KEYWORDS: publishing, history of the book, history of wales, welsh language, history of printing

ISBNs: 9781108948173 (PB), 9781108951159 (OC)
ISSNs: 2514-8524 (online), 2514-8516 (print)

Contents

1 Introduction

I believe that nothing will invigorate the Welshman's character as much as the knowledge of his own country's history. —Owen M. Edwards[1]

Over the past 1,500 years, Welsh writers have produced some of the greatest works of literature and poetry. Their contributions have, as Welsh poet Dylan Thomas wrote, "change[d] the shape of the universe" (Thomas, 1991: 61). But all of those contributions have been made possible by the physical labor of publishing – the tedious repetition of handwriting manuscripts by medieval monks, the backbreaking work of printing on a Gutenberg-style press, the lightning-fast printing of the industrial age, and the new challenges of paperless electronic publishing.

The creation of texts – whether handwritten, printed, or electronic – preserves culture, literature, myths, and society, and provides invaluable insights into history. Yet, with all of the billions of texts that have been produced, we still have much to learn about the history of how those texts were produced and preserved by the publishing process, and how the production of texts has influenced modern societies. In a letter to his wife in 1936, Thomas wrote, "Our discreditable secret is that we don't know anything at all, and our horrid inner secret is that we don't care that we don't" (Ferris, 1985: 242). In studies of the history of publishing, the number of things we don't know is sometimes the dark secret. Courses and published histories cover the major developments – a broad outline of publishing, printing, and papers from ancient Egypt, Han dynasty China, and medieval Arabia and Europe through Johannes Gutenberg, William Caxton, and Lord Stanhope – without necessarily delving into the smaller implementations of publishing that have shaped the histories of nations, peoples, cultures, and languages. Understanding these smaller publishing efforts provides greater impact and depth to the history of publishing: studying a small-town printer in nineteenth-century Wales who created local newsletters and religious pamphlets provides powerful evidence of the long-term reach of Gutenberg's innovations.

[1] Walters, 1998: 206.

For many small nations around the world, publishing is tied together in the history of the people – revolutions, renaissance, resistance, and resurgence. Culture, history, and texts are inextricably connected, making the printed word a good window into the world of those nations. Like other small nations, Wales has a long history with texts, going back to at least Roman Britain. Wales differs from other small nations, however, in two significant ways. First, the Welsh people maintained a primarily oral culture into the 1700s, centuries after the arrival of books in Britain. Second, Wales coexists on the same small island as two powerful publishing centers – Edinburgh and London – and its own history of publishing in the post-Gutenberg era has been constrained by location, restrictive publishing laws, and the English suppression of Welsh language and culture. As a result, publishing history in Wales has been overshadowed by the histories of its larger neighbors. These differences contribute to (1) a total volume of Welsh books that is much smaller than other nations, particularly before 1700 and (2) an underexplored history of publishing in Wales. As we dig into the history, we find that the few texts that do exist are deeply intertwined with the history, culture, myths, and language of Wales.

The story of publishing in Wales, then, is closely connected to the story of Wales itself – a long history of a remarkably resilient culture with roots in the ancient history of the British Isles. Wales, the Welsh people, and the Welsh language have survived invasion, migration, oppression, revolt, resistance, religious and social upheavals, and economic depression. The books of Wales chronicle this story and the Welsh people's endurance over centuries of challenges. Ancient law books, medieval manuscripts, legends and myths, secretly printed religious works, poetry, song, social commentary, and modern novels tell a story of a tiny nation, its hardy people, and an enduring literary legacy that has an outsized influence on culture and literature far beyond the Welsh borders.

At this point, some readers may echo Sir Thomas More's sentiment in Robert Bolt's *A Man for All Seasons*, "For Wales? Why Richard, it profit a man nothing to give his soul for the whole world . . . but for Wales!" (Bolt, 2013: 120). The answer to this question has two parts: First, in spite of its small size, Wales has been a major contributor to world culture, particularly in the English-speaking world. Welsh histories and myths provide the foundation of Arthurian legend and other British mythologies; Welsh-born monarchs transformed England into a world power; and Welsh literature, poetry, and song have spread throughout the world. Second, a serious exploration of publishing in Wales is valuable to the Welsh people as a record of their turbulent history and a testament to their endurance as a culturally distinct group.

Some studies of publishing history, such as John Feather's *A History of British Publishing* or Colin Clair's *A History of European Printing*, contain only passing references to publishing in Wales, usually as a very minor subset of the British market. Many histories of publishing make no mention of Wales at all, except perhaps in footnotes. In the past few decades, however, there has been a growing body of scholarship on the unique aspects of publishing in Wales. The valuable collection *A Nation and Its Books*, edited by Jones and Rees, provides a detailed examination of the history and issues associated with Welsh publishing, while *The Cambridge History of Welsh Literature*, edited by Evans and Fulton, examines the vital role of literature and texts in Wales since Roman times. Larger collections, including the impressive multivolume set *The Cambridge History of the Book in Britain*, treat Wales as an important contributor to British publishing while recognizing the unique – and separate – publishing history of Wales. In this Element, the goal is to provide a brief, accessible overview of Welsh publishing in the context of the history of Wales.

The Element provides an outline of the history of publishing in Wales, from its earliest beginnings in the Roman era through the digital publishing efforts of the twenty-first century. It will begin with a brief review of the history of Wales, focusing on the major events that shaped the unique identity of Welsh culture. It will then examine Welsh publishing history in five eras: from early literacy through medieval manuscript production (ancient history through 1450), early Welsh printing (1450–1718), Industrial Age publishing (1718–1847), Welsh Renaissance (1847–1992), and the electronic age (1992–present). Each of these eras is bounded by an important event that shaped publishing history in Wales: the invention of the Gutenberg press in 1450 (although printing didn't come to the British Isles until several decades later); the establishment of the first legal printing press in Wales in 1718; the release of *Reports of the Commissioners of Enquiry into the State of Education in Wales*, more commonly known as the Parliamentary Blue Books, in 1847; and the recognition of the Welsh language as an official language in 1993.

Of course, in attempting to create an overview of a history as long and complex as that of Welsh publishing, there are bound to be complications. One of these complications is the definition of Welsh publishing itself. Although the title of this Element is *Publishing in Wales*, the complicated history of Wales and its interactions with its neighbors in Britain means there are really four different aspects of publishing that need to be explored:

1. *Books in Wales*. Like most European countries, Wales has a tradition of books that predates printing by several centuries. The ancient handwritten books of Wales preserve the law, culture, language, stories, poems, and traditions of the Welsh people from before the advent of printing. These books provide important evidence of the history and culture of the British Isles from pre-Roman times through the Norman Conquest.

2. *Publishing in Welsh*. Although we know that the Welsh language likely predates the Roman presence in Britain, the earliest manuscript in Welsh is preserved in the marginalia of Latin manuscripts in the 900s. Welsh has always been sidelined or suppressed as a secondary language for publishing in the British Isles from the time of the Roman invasion. The language has persevered, however, and Welsh authors began publishing in their native tongue from the earliest days of printing, in spite of official opposition and logistical difficulties.

3. *Publishing by Welsh authors*. Some of the most significant contributions in Welsh publishing history were made by Welsh authors who wrote and published in other languages: Latin, Old English, French, and English. Welsh scribes copied the Gospels; Welsh historians documented the early history of Britain; Welsh poets recorded the epics and myths of the British Isles; Welsh lyricists contributed songs to the Protestant hymnal; and Welsh authors have continued to shape the poems, songs, and literature of the post-Gutenberg world.

4. *Publishing in Wales*. The origins of printing in Wales are much later than most of the rest of Europe. English laws forbade printing outside of the approved presses in London until the 1700s. While some printing was done in secret in Wales, the advent of a publishing industry was delayed

until laws were relaxed in the 1700s. In the nineteenth and twentieth centuries, civil, political, social, and religious unrest was connected to a small but important printing industry in Wales.

These four aspects of publishing in Wales come together with intertwining stories that grow together to create a bigger picture of a publishing industry vital to culture, language, and identity in Wales. This Element attempts to capture that bigger picture and to show its connection with and importance to the worldwide history of publishing.

The other complication with creating a history of Welsh publishing is that Wales is a small nation with a small number of publications. For all of the Welsh contributions to the world, we simply have a much smaller library of texts – manuscripts, books, and other publications – on which we rely to tell the story. For example, in the sixteenth century, the total number of books printed in Europe and Great Britain was over 200 million, and that number increased to more than half a billion in the seventeenth century, representing hundreds of thousands of individual titles (Roser, 2013). By contrast, "the number of Welsh books of all kinds printed during the sixteenth century was only thirty, with a further 150 in the seventeenth century" (Williams, 1998: 49).

While working with a much smaller data set is difficult, it also allows for more individual stories to be told. Each book, after all, is the culmination of the work of the author and all the people associated with printing the book. Throughout this Element, I include some of these individual stories and focus on some of the important publications in Wales and the people who produced them. These individual stories, as distant descendants of the rich Welsh storytelling tradition, help create a broad overview of Welsh publishing history.

2 Welsh History and Identity

If, therefore, they would be inseparable, they would become insuperable.
—Gerald of Wales[2]

Modern Wales is a small nation of idyllic landscapes, resort towns, and agriculture that also bears the scars of industrialization and the postindustrial economic slump. Wales is bounded on the west by the Irish Sea and on the east by Offa's Dyke, and its hills are dotted with crumbling Norman castles, great manor houses, quarries, and mines. The Welsh landscape tells part of the story of this nation and its resilient people, who are often forgotten or subsumed into their membership in the United Kingdom.

But the rest of the story is told in the books of Wales. As "one of the oldest continuous literary traditions in Europe" (Evans and Fulton, 2019: i), the books of Wales establish and maintain the unique Welsh identity. Welsh people are distinct, culturally and linguistically – the proud descendants of ancient Celts who have survived waves of migration and invasion by Romans, Anglo-Saxons, Vikings, and Normans, and have preserved their identity through history, poetry, song, and story. There could be many approaches to a brief historical overview of Wales, but in this Element, I focus on three aspects of Welsh identity: (1) the existence of Wales as a separate nation, (2) the independence of the Welsh religion, and (3) the endurance of the Welsh language. Each of these aspects came under attack during each invasion of Wales, particularly in the Tudor era, and the Welsh responses have shaped the history of Welsh publishing.

2.1 Wales as a Separate Nation

The Welsh are not like any other people in Britain, and they know how separate they are. They are the Celts, the tough little wine-dark race who were the original possessors of the island, who never mixed with the invaders coming later from the east, but were slowly driven into the western mountains.
—Laurie Lee[3]

---

[2] Cambrensis, 2018: 39. [3] Lee, 2015.

Wales has existed as an identifiable geographical area since the mid-700s when Offa, the king of Mercia, ordered the construction of a miles-long earthwork to mark the boundary between his Anglo-Saxon kingdom and the Welsh kingdom of Powys to the West. But the eighth-century Welsh princes connected their traditions, language, and culture to the Britons, who had ruled the island for centuries before the Romans invaded. Nineteenth-century Welsh writers connected the settlement of Wales even further back to the time of the biblical flood. The idea of Wales as a separate nation, rooted in biblical mythology, "became part of the warp and woof of the cultural experience of the Welsh people" (Jenkins, 2007: 5).

The archeological records tell a different, but no less fascinating, story. Although there were inhabitants of the British Isles dating back to Ice Age hunters, the story of Wales begins when the earliest Celts arrived around 600 BCE, bringing with them a powerful Iron Age civilization with extensive ties to the European continent and an "extraordinary material culture" (Jenkins, 2007: 18). Archeological records show that these early Celts traded goods with their Celtic cousins in Europe and, later, with the Greeks, Etruscans, and Romans.

The Celtic migration to the British Isles was significant for at least two reasons. First, the Celtic immigrants created the culture, languages, and legacy of ancient Britain and became the foundation of the people in the areas that became Wales, Scotland, and Ireland. Second, the Celtic emphasis on travel and trade brought the British Isles to the attention of the growing European civilizations and began a series of invasions, migrations, and cultural and social upheavals.

The first major challenge to the Celtic civilizations came in 55 BCE when Julius Caesar began the Roman invasion of Britain. Caesar's invasion brought the island under nominal Roman control, but there wasn't a military presence and the Celtic tribes remained autonomous – as long as they paid tributes of goods and slaves to Rome. Later invasions "undertaken by the most stupid, maintained by the most dissolute, and terminated by the most timid of all the emperors" (Smith, 1874: 2) finally brought Britain under Roman control by the end of the first century CE. The Romans held the south and east, while the Celts were pushed to the west into Wales and to the north into Scotland, establishing centers of resistance that the Romans never fully conquered.

The Romans brought trade, prosperity, and Roman culture to the island. They built villas, amphitheaters, roads, aqueducts, and fortified walls. Roman citizens intermarried with the Celtic inhabitants, and Celtic rulers sent their children to Rome to be educated in Latin, undergo training in Roman warfare, and form critical political alliances. Rather than being absorbed into Roman culture, however, the Britons in Wales developed a linguistic and cultural identity with ties to both the independent Celts and the classical Romans. This Romano-British culture set them apart from both the Romans and their Celtic cousins to the north.

In subsequent centuries, the Romano-British legacy became romanticized in legend and song as the ideal of the British character, which is a study in contrasts between the cultures – the rugged hardiness of the Celts and the classical civilization of the Romans, the magical traditions of the British Isles and the miracle-based faith of Christianity, the terrifying blue-painted Celtic armies and the ordered ranks of Roman legions. This ideal and the conflicts surrounding it were preserved in bardic ballads and became the foundation of Welsh mythologies, including *The Mabinogion* and the legends of King Arthur.

The decline of the Roman Empire opened the door for the Germanic tribes who were spreading all over Europe. In roughly 450 CE, several Germanic tribes, including Angles, Jutes, Saxons, Frisii, and Franks, began to arrive in the British Isles. Unlike the Roman Conquest, the Germanic settlement was more of a centuries-long migration to the island where Anglo-Saxons gradually replaced the language and culture with their own – at least in England. In Wales and Scotland, the well-established Celtic kingdoms were joined by the Romano-British people who were pushed out of the south and east by the Germanic invaders.

Once again, Wales and Scotland were the centers of resistance to the newest inhabitants of Britain. Wales was ruled by princes (from the Latin *principus*, a title the Welsh rulers preferred to the title *king*, from the Proto-Germanic *kuningaʐ* [Davies, 2007a: 69–70]) who rivaled the Anglo-Saxon kings in power and influence. By the mid- to late 500s, Wales was divided into several small kingdoms with flexible borders that usually (but certainly not always) stood together against the growing Anglo-Saxon kingdoms of Mercia and Wessex. Over the next two centuries, the Welsh kingdoms repelled repeated invasions from the east and took advantage of conflicts between the Anglo-Saxon rulers to maintain Welsh autonomy.

By the late 700s, all of the kingdoms of medieval Britain – the Welsh, the Anglo-Saxon, and the Scottish – faced a new threat. Viking raiders began attacking the coasts, sacking monasteries and towns, and establishing settlements. These new incursions set off a fresh round of violence within Britain. Internal struggles among rival Welsh princes and conflicts among the Anglo-Saxon rulers, combined with the ongoing threat of Danish invasion, led to civil wars and general strife throughout the island.

In 886, Alfred, the king of the West Saxons, declared himself king of the Anglo-Saxons after a series of decisive victories over rival Anglo-Saxon kings and the Danes. Alfred's power over the Anglo-Saxon kingdoms and ability to resist the Vikings made him an attractive ally for the Welsh princes. When Alfred proclaimed himself king of the Anglo-Saxons, several of the Welsh princes swore fealty to him, which brought most of Wales under Anglo-Saxon rule for the first time.

Alfred's death in 899 did not signal the end of the unified kingdom of England. It did, however, end the alliance with the Welsh princes. By 900, Wales was once again independent, dominated by the powerful Anarawd ap Rhodri of Gwynedd, who had used his friendship with Alfred to cement his own authority over his brothers' kingdoms of Ceredigion and Powys. This arrangement of a unified England sharing an uneasy border with the powerful Welsh kingdoms continued until William of Normandy landed in England in 1066 and defeated Harold Godwinson – the last Anglo-Saxon king.

The Norman Conquest was more complete than any of the invasions before it. As William wrote in his deathbed confession:

> I persecuted the native inhabitants of England beyond
> all reason. Whether nobles or commons, I cruelly
> oppressed them; many I unjustly disinherited; innumerable

> multitudes ... perished through me by famine and sword ...
> I am stained with the rivers of blood that I have shed.
>
> (quoted in Wood, n.d.)

Through massive waves of violence, the Normans went beyond gaining land and achieving control. They replaced large parts of the society. Anglo-Saxon lords were stripped of their titles and went into hiding, while William rewarded his followers with lands and titles. Norman castles were built throughout Britain, designed as visible shows of dominance as much as for defense. Norman French replaced Old English as the language of the elite, and Norman laws and customs were patched over the existing Anglo-Saxon laws.

Although England fell to William fairly quickly, the Celtic fringe proved much more difficult. The Welsh princes were powerful, and they had centuries of experience in defending their borders from encroaching armies. Although the Normans enjoyed initial success in their invasions, the Welsh princes resisted, and by 1100, most of Wales was back under Welsh control. But, similar to their struggles against the Anglo-Saxons, the Welsh kingdoms were unable to completely unite against the Normans. Succession crises and infighting led some of the Welsh princes to make alliances with the Normans; some, like Owain ap Cadwgan, were even knighted for their service to the English king.

As part of his initial attempt to conquer Wales, William installed a number of lords along the border to guard it and to take as much of Wales as they could. These Marcher Lords (*march* in this case means "border" or "boundary") were given far more power than the other Norman nobility. They could build their own castles, rule according to their own laws (which were often a combination of Norman laws and the ancient Welsh law *Cyfraith Hywel*), and mount military campaigns – all without the approval of the king. The Marcher Lords intermarried with the Welsh princely families, creating a Norman-Welsh nobility that was beholden to the king of England and allied with the great families of Wales. The hope on the part of the king was that the Marcher Lords could control the Welsh and eventually conquer Wales, through force, by marriage, or by inheritance.

But it was not to be. Even with their growing connections to England, the Welsh people were fiercely independent. In *Descriptio Cambriae*, written in 1194, Gerald of Wales quotes one old Welshman's message for King Henry II:

> My Lord King, this nation may now be harassed, weakened and decimated by your soldiery, as it has so often been by others in former times; but it will never be totally destroyed by the wrath of man, unless at the same time it is punished by the wrath of God. Whatever else may come to pass, I do not think that on the Day of Direst Judgement any race other than the Welsh, or any other language, will give answer to the Supreme Judge of all for this small corner of the earth.
>
> (Gerald of Wales, 1997a)

By this time, a large part of the Welsh identity was tied to the people's ability to repel invasions and endure as a separate culture. Frankly, centuries of evidence was on their side. Welsh armies had held back waves of invading Romans, Anglo-Saxons, and Vikings for a thousand years; they believed they could resist the Normans. But the Normans were more persistent, more aggressive, and more powerful than their previous foes.

Over the two centuries following the Norman Conquest, control of the kingdoms in Wales passed back and forth between the English crown and the Welsh princes. Llywelyn the Great gained extraordinary power over Wales in about 1200, only to have his dynasty fall apart after his death. A few decades later, Edward I of England invaded Wales and began full-scale oppression of the Welsh people. He placed restrictions on Welsh movements, laws, and language and built several massive castles to house his troops and solidify his control. He even organized for his infant son to be born at Caernarfon to fulfill a promise that the next Prince of Wales would be "borne in Wales and could speake never a word of English" (Powel, quoted in Cull, 2014: 39). Edward's son was named the Prince of Wales, beginning a long tradition of English princes with that title and effectively ending the Welsh hope of self-government (Davies, 2007a: 175).

Nearly a century after the oppressions of Edward I, the last great Welsh revolt began under one of the most important Welsh heroes, Owain Glyndŵr.

Glyndŵr was a Marcher Lord, but he was also descended from the royal houses of three Welsh kingdoms – Powys, Deheubarth, and Gwynedd – and a direct descendant of Llywelyn the Great. Glyndŵr had the pedigree and the will to make a last stand for Welsh sovereignty. In 1400, Owain Glyndŵr opened a war with the English, fueled by the Welsh nationalist drive for independence. Glyndŵr's military successes, connected with the English Parliament's attempts to stem the rebellion by tightening laws in 1402, drove more Welsh citizens to support Glyndŵr's campaign. Laborers, students, and nobility left England to return to Wales and join the rebellion.

In 1404, Glyndŵr convened a Welsh parliament, was crowned the Prince of Wales, and controlled most of the country. But by 1409, he had lost everything: his territory was back in English hands, his family taken to the Tower of London, and his soldiers dead or deserted. In 1412, Glyndŵr led one final successful raid at Brecon and then disappeared. Although there are rumors and legends after 1412, no one really knows where the last Welsh Prince of Wales went or when and where he died. In Welsh legend, Owain Glyndŵr continues to roam the hills and will return, like King Arthur, to once again unite the Welsh in independence.

Although Owain Glyndŵr was ultimately defeated, his family continued to have a huge effect on the entire island of Britain. In 1485, after decades of civil war in England, Henry Tudor defeated King Richard III at the Battle of Bosworth Field and took the crown as King Henry VII. Henry was a descendant of both English royalty and Welsh royalty, specifically the Tudors of Penmynydd, who were cousins of Owain Glyndŵr and who had participated in his revolt against the English. The Tudors mark a turning point in Welsh and British history, not just for the independence of the Welsh people but also for their religion and language.

2.2 Religion in Wales

There is, I believe, no part of the nation more inclined to be religious, and to be delighted with it than the poor inhabitants of these mountains.

—Erasmus Saunders[4]

---

[4] Jenkins, 1998: 14.

Welsh religious independence goes back to the earliest history of Britain when the Celtic tribes refused to adopt the religion of the invading Romans. The Roman connection to Europe, however, connected the Celtic tribes to early Christians. Legends say that Lucius, the king of the Britons, sent a letter to Pope Eleutherius in about 180 CE asking to convert to Christianity after he heard of the miraculous works of Christian disciples in Europe. The pope assented, and Lucius was baptized. His conversion led to the Christianization of Lucius's entire kingdom and eventually the conversion of most of the other Celtic kingdoms. Very little contemporary evidence exists about Lucius, and he may be a medieval creation based on earlier myths. There is ample evidence, however, that the Celtic kingdoms converted to Christianity nearly 200 years before Emperor Constantine led the Roman Empire into the religion.

Over the next several centuries, Christianity thrived in the Celtic kingdoms, even during the Diocletian suppression, where Christians throughout the Roman Empire were slaughtered and oppressed. Celtic Christianity survived and developed its own characteristics, with distinctive art, architecture, and holy days. Significantly, ancient Celtic mythologies began to be transformed from the worship of a pantheon of gods to the veneration of Christian monarchs. Ancient gods became mythic kings, and traditional magic became Christian miracles. Jenkins argues: "Indeed, there are strong grounds for believing that the spread of Christianity helped to develop a distinctive Welsh identity. The Welsh began to see themselves as a largely Christian people who, set apart from the ruffianly Anglo-Saxon pagans, were therefore culturally superior" (Jenkins, 2007: 55). As the Roman Catholic Church grew in power, attempts were made to unify and standardize Christian worship. Welsh Christianity remained stubbornly unique, however, with its own versions of the sacraments and its own calendar of holy days. It wasn't until 768 that Celtic practices were fully replaced by Roman Catholic rites, and even then there remained in Wales a culture of religious independence that continued through subsequent invasions and religious changes, including the reforms and religious oppressions of the Tudor monarchs.

2.3 The Welsh Language

If you do not wish to become worse than animals . . . insist on learning in your
language: and if you do not wish to be more unnatural than any other nation
under the sun, love your language and those who love it.

– William Salesbury[5]

The third element of Welsh identity is the language. While Wales lost its geopolitical independence to Edward I and its religious uniqueness to the spread of Catholicism, it maintained the Welsh language, even as the languages of the rest of the British Isles were replaced and adapted by the various waves of invasions. Welsh traces its roots to the earliest Celtic languages, which over time split into two broad language families: the Brittonic (often called Brythonic or Brythoneg in Welsh) and the Gaelic (sometimes called Goidelic). These families are the predecessors of modern Celtic languages in Britain, with Brittonic being the ancestor of Welsh, Cornish, Breton, and Cumbric; and Gaelic being the ancestor of Irish, Scottish Gaelic, and Manx.

During Roman rule, Welsh rulers spoke and wrote in Latin, but the primary language of their people was Brittonic, which evolved into primitive Welsh by about the sixth century. As the Anglo-Saxons and the Vikings invaded, bringing linguistic changes to the rest of Britain, Welsh continued to develop on its own, creating a unique enclave of the ancient tongue as England moved toward English.

One of the early major challenges to Welsh as a language was the rule of Alfred the Great (d. 899 CE). Alfred's focus on education in his kingdom was a major step toward the dominance of the English language. Alfred gathered scholars and books from the major learning centers, including St. Davids in Wales, and with their help introduced public education to England. In addition, during Alfred's reign an increasing number of books were written in Old English rather than Latin, which also called into question the place of the Welsh language in society. Alfred's rule was a major step toward the elevation of the English language that happened over the next several centuries until the Tudor monarchs entrenched English in the law.

---

[5] Price, 2019: 181.

Even as English became the standard throughout Britain, however, Welsh was maintained, not simply as a language, but as a deeply symbolic connection to Welsh identity. Angharad Price wrote, "At precisely the moment when Wales's political identity was being subsumed into Tudor England, the Welsh humanists made their own vernacular a powerful means of expressing cultural sovereignty" (Price, 2019: 191). The Tudor oppression was followed by subsequent efforts to eliminate Welsh, but in each effort the Welsh people have refused to relinquish the language that is key to Welsh identity.

2.4 Reforms, Oppressions, and Revolts

Whoever leads an auspicious life here and governs the commonwealth rightly, as my most noble father did, who promoted all piety and banished all ignorance, has a most certain way to heaven.

—Henry VIII[6]

The Tudor dynasty began a series of massive changes for society, religion, and language throughout Britain. Henry VII was the last of the English monarchs to win his crown on the battlefield. He also began a series of major reforms to government and society in Britain that were continued and expanded by his descendants. As William Campbell wrote:

> By Henry VII, the sword of government was sheathed, the remains of the feudal system at last completely swept away, the undue domination of the nobles set aside to make room for the growing influence of the mighty middle class, in which our modern civilization, with its faults and its merits, has established its stronghold. (Campbell, 2012: ix)

On the surface, having a Welsh dynasty seems like it would be a good thing for Wales. In reality, it was a mixed bag. After centuries of revolts, suppression, and immigration, the Welsh were ready for peace and, even

---

[6] Parr, 2011: 129.

more, ready for integration. The Tudor monarchs advanced the integration of Wales into England through reform of the government, laws, and relationships between the two nations. While this was a period of internal peace in the English territories, it was also a period of oppression and subjugation.

King Henry VIII's reign was marked by a number of reforms as the king worked to increase his own power over the entire kingdom. In 1534, Henry was declared head of the English Church by the Acts of Supremacy. In 1535, the autonomy of Welsh territories and the Marcher Lords were ended by the first Laws in Wales Act, which said: "That his said Country or Dominion of Wales shall be, stand and continue for ever from henceforth incorporated, united and annexed to and with this his Realm of England" (*Laws in Wales Act*, 1535). Welsh laws, which had been the governing force since they were written down in *Cyfraith Hywel* during the reign of Hywel Dda (d. 948 CE), were finally replaced by the Laws in Wales Act of 1542. And, most importantly, the acts made English the only official language with the stipulation that "from henceforth no Person or Persons that use the Welch Speech or Language, shall have or enjoy any manner Office or Fees within this Realm of England, Wales, or other the King's Dominion, upon Pain of forfeiting the same Offices or Fees, unless he or they use and exercise the English Speech or Language" (*Laws in Wales Act*, 1542).

Henry VIII's reforms were designed to unify England and Wales and to forestall future rebellions against the crown. By annexing Wales officially and eliminating autonomous lordships, Henry was building a new nation based on a strong monarch and a single central parliament. This, combined with the transition away from the Catholic Pope in Rome, created the foundations of the British Empire and the modern United Kingdom. It was, however, particularly hard on the Welsh people. In the Laws in Wales acts, Henry was pushing for national, religious, and linguistic unity, while the Welsh were a separate country dominated by Catholics who spoke Welsh rather than English. Already seen as rebellious and troublesome, the Welsh were now cast as treasonous for their national identity, culture, language, and religion.

On the other hand, by the reign of the Tudors, the Welsh people were more ready to integrate with the English. Centuries of conflict and settlement had mixed the populations: the Welsh nobility had deep ties to the English crown, and the Welsh populace was intermixed with the Anglo-Norman settlers who were sent by Edward I. While Welsh remained an important language of the country, many of the people spoke English as well, especially those in the noble and merchant classes. English language and English society came to be seen as markers of the elite, while the older Welsh language and culture were often presented as backward in English-language materials.

Official English suppression of Wales continued after the Tudor dynasty was replaced by the Stuarts and through the English Civil Wars. In the 1650s, Parliament passed a series of acts to strengthen English rule in Wales. Among other things, these acts punished Catholics by removing them from their government positions and other appointments and putting some of them under house arrest. In addition, the acts established schools for teaching English and the Gospel of the Church of England. Catholic influence and the Welsh language waned as they were slowly replaced by the Anglican Communion and English.

The Tudor period also saw the beginning of new industries in Wales – industries that formed the foundation of the Welsh economy until the twentieth century. In 1584, the first major Welsh copper smelting works was established, and it was soon followed by iron works. Although the metal works factories brought major economic benefits to Wales, they were often run by English owners and they employed many workers who came to Wales from Dublin, London, and Liverpool. The early days of the metal works industry set the stage for a large working class in Wales with a mixture of Welsh, Irish, and English heritage.

Within two centuries, Wales became a major producer of another vital mineral: coal. As Britain geared up for the Industrial Revolution, the coal mines in Wales expanded, providing new jobs in mines, processing facilities, and support industries. Like the earlier copper and iron works, these mines were generally owned by the wealthy elite in London. The money generated by the coal mines flowed out of Wales, leaving the Welsh people impoverished and oppressed. In addition, several large-scale mining accidents and explosions in the mid- to late-1800s killed hundreds of workers and severely damaged the industry. Nevertheless, the coal mining industry continued to grow, and at its peak, employed more than 230,000 men in Wales and many more in support industries (Davies, 2007a: 476).

The combination of poverty, ongoing oppression of the Welsh people, terrible working conditions, and changing political and social structures made conditions ripe for violence and political and social upheaval. Beginning in 1831, there were full-scale revolts by the working class in Merthyr Tydfil, then the largest city in Wales and the center of the mining industry. Additional revolts followed, including the Newport Rising in 1839 and the Rebecca Riots in 1842. The unrest was focused on clashes between the working classes and those they saw as oppressors: mine owners, management, the educated and elite, and government officials.

The protests in Industrial Wales were ended violently by British troops. In the Merthyr Rising, twenty-four protesters were killed; in the Newport Rising, which involved over 4,000 demonstrators, another twenty-two were killed. The leaders of the various protests were imprisoned or transported, and one, Richard Lewis, was hanged (Davies, 2007a: 356–57). This unrest in Wales did lead to some reforms in working conditions and in worker rights. Just as important, however, the protests were an early part of a Welsh Renaissance of poetry, literature, and song in both English and Welsh, based on a revived sense of Welsh nationalism.

2.5 Modern Wales

Daeth gwanwyn yn hwyr i'n gwlad;	*Spring came late to our country;*
y gaea wedi cloi ein huchelgais	*the winter locked down ambition*
a gwydro ein dyheadau,	*and put our aspirations on ice,*
cyn y dadmer mawr,	*before the big thaw*
a barodd i'r gwteri garglo	*which made the drains gargle*
a'r landeri garlamu.	*and the downpipes gush.*

– Ifor ap Glyn[7]

---

[7] Glyn, 2016.

After the violence in Wales during the first half of the nineteenth century, the nation settled into a relative calm. Its coal mines and steel works helped to power the machines of the expanding British Empire, and the Welsh economy relied almost exclusively on those industries. Welsh nationalism, driven by the divisive *Reports of the Commissioners of Enquiry into the State of Education in Wales*, published in 1847, involved a push for the recognition of the Welsh language and requests for more autonomy and self-government.

As difficult as the process of industrialization had been on Wales in the eighteenth and nineteenth centuries, the many changes in the twentieth century were perhaps even more difficult. Two world wars decimated the ranks of the young working class, and the steep decline of the coal and steel industries after World War II eroded the Welsh economy.

But there were wins, as well. After centuries of official suppression of Welsh resulted in near extinction of the language, the political party Plaid Cymru was formed in 1925 to promote and preserve Welsh. Plaid Cymru campaigned for Welsh broadcasts on radio and television, Welsh-language newspapers, and the teaching of Welsh in primary schools. Continued Welsh activism eventually led to the British Government easing the restrictions on Welsh, first in the Welsh Language Act of 1967, which allowed Welsh to be used in some government documents and court proceedings and then the Welsh Language Act of 1993, which officially made Welsh equal to English for the first time since the mid-1500s.

Wales made political gains, as well, with the establishment of the Welsh Assembly in 1999, and the National Assembly for Wales in 2006 (now called *Senedd Cymru*, or "Welsh Parliament"), which provided some political autonomy for the small nation. In the twenty-first century, Welsh lawmakers are once again making decisions for Wales in Welsh. Welsh identity as a separate nation with its own language and a uniquely Welsh approach to religion – as documented in centuries of its books – has once again come to the forefront.

3 Poetry, Literacy, and Manuscripts

*The transference of oral tradition to writing and print does not destroy its
validity as folklore but rather, while freezing or fixing its form, helps to keep
it alive and to diffuse it among those to whom it is not native or fundamental.*
                                                              – B. A. Botkin[8]

Publishing in its modern form – the production, printing, and distribution
of books and other texts – came to Wales much later than the rest of the
British Isles and most of Europe. This delay was due to Parliamentary
suppression of Welsh culture, language, and texts, which continued in
different forms and under various laws from the reign of Edward I in the
late 1200s through the official recognition of the Welsh language in 1993.

But the lack of an in-country publishing infrastructure did not stop
Welsh contributions. Whether they were printing on the Stationers' presses
in London or Oxford, European presses, or illegal presses, Welsh authors
and poets found ways to build a publishing culture out of an already strong
literate culture based on ancient Welsh traditions, poetry, songs, histories,
and laws. Like the origins of publishing in most countries, the story of
publishing in Wales begins centuries before the advent of printing with the
oral traditions and handwritten manuscripts of the early Welsh.

3.1 Bardic Traditions

Diwedd y gân yw'r geiniog

(At the end of the song comes payment)
                    —Welsh Proverb[9]

The pre-Roman Celtic settlements in the British Isles relied on a well-
developed oral culture. Like other early civilizations, the Celts tracked histories, repeated myths, crafted poetry, wove epics, and sang songs. Unlike
many other European cultures, the Welsh focus on orality – sometimes at the

[8] Botkin, 1996: 256. [9] Hemmings, 2019.

expense of the written word – has continued to play a dominant role in the country's production and preservation of Welsh culture. Even into the seventeenth and eighteenth centuries, the primary transmission of the great works of Welsh culture was through oral repetition (Pryce, 1998: 8–9). The focus on orality over literacy became a distinguishing feature of the Welsh that set them apart from the other groups in the British Isles, who transitioned to text-based cultures much earlier.

One of the major reasons that the Welsh oral traditions continued into modern times was the prominent role of the bards in Welsh society. Initially, bards were professional poets who worked for the Celtic princes, composing eulogies and epics to memorialize – or parodize, depending on the reputation and generosity of the clients – the exploits of the rulers. In addition, the bards kept the complex genealogies of the royal houses, and would recite them at official events. The bards enjoyed a unique and important role in Welsh society, and some of them, such as Taliesin and Aneirin, became the subject of Welsh legends themselves.

The history and legends of Wales were preserved primarily by the bards, and later medieval writers relied heavily on these oral traditions (with a healthy dose of creative license) to write their manuscripts. Because they worked for the Welsh princes, the bards tended to compose verses that showcased their employers' legitimate claims to the throne through connection to historical figures and divine or supernatural abilities. Our understanding of Welsh history and its legends, including the medieval manuscripts of the *Mabinogion, Historia Brittonum, Historia Regum Brittaniae*, and various Arthurian epics, comes from the bardic traditions.

One of the enduring legacies of the bardic tradition is the *eisteddfod*. This Welsh cultural and literary festival originated in gatherings of the bards to showcase their songs and poetry. In post-Roman Wales, eisteddfodau (*eisteddfodau* is the Welsh plural, which is used more frequently than the Anglicized *eisteddfods*) were sponsored by the royal houses and became one of the ways that a Welsh prince could demonstrate his power. The bards would sing old songs and new compositions and the best were awarded with honor and prizes. Eisteddfodau continued as a regular feature of Welsh society until the Edwardian oppression of the 1300s, when the Welsh princes were replaced by English lords and the royal bardic tradition ended. Even then, the bards and the eisteddfodau continued, though in a much-diminished role. Both the bards and the eisteddfodau were funded by the remnants of the Welsh nobility, the Anglo-Welsh Marcher lords, or the more wealthy members of Welsh society, and for the most part, they focused on local communities (see Edwards, 2019: 287–88). National eisteddfodau were not reinstated until the reigns of the Welsh Tudor kings in the 1500s. Modern celebrations of the eisteddfod, including the National Eisteddfod of Wales, are the results of an eighteenth-century revival of the bardic culture.

The bards were just one part of the oral tradition in Wales, however. There is ample evidence that poetry and song permeated Welsh society from early in the country's history. Welsh poets developed their own form of unique poetry, with specific meters and rhyme schemes, that have endured for more than a millennium. The first written examples of Welsh poetry show up in the marginalia of Latin manuscripts in the mid-900s, but by that point they already demonstrate a well-developed and consistent poetic form. In 1194, Gerald of Wales described Welsh poetry in his *Descriptio Cambriae*:

> In their rhymed songs and set speeches they are so subtle and ingenious that they produce, in their native tongue, ornaments of wonderful and exquisite invention both in the words and the sentences . . . They make use of alliteration in preference to all other ornaments of rhetoric, and that particular kind which joins by consonancy the first letters or syllables of words.
>
> (Cambrensis, 2018: 18)

The recorded poetry and songs of the Welsh bards provides the earliest glimpse into Welsh culture after the fall of Rome, but it also makes studying that period a little tricky. The bardic tradition made history, legend, stories, and genealogies the realm of the poets, rather than that of the writers. This focus on oral transmission of Welsh culture affects what has been preserved in ancient Welsh books. Rather than preserving the great stories, songs, and history of a people, early medieval Welsh books focus instead on religion, law, property, diplomacy, and war.

3.2 Early Literacy

The origins of literacy in Wales are to be sought in the Romano-British Church.
—Huw Pryce[10]

The Celtic lands are dotted with pre-Roman monuments and artwork on stones and tombs. These ancient writing systems provide evidence of some literacy, at least in the ruling or priestly classes of the early Celts. The practice of monumental stonework continued through the Roman period and into the early medieval era, albeit with a distinctly Christian turn after around 200–300 CE. For the first few hundred years of literacy in Wales, the primary surviving documents are these monumental stones engraved in Irish or Latin, with many of the stones including both languages. These stones show links to broader Christianity, particularly the churches in Ireland and in Gaul, but they also provide evidence that "those responsible for erecting the monuments ... valued the written word" (Pryce, 1998: 4).

The monumental stones show the earliest signs of literacy in Wales, but the advent of Christianity brought with it written manuscripts and books from the Roman tradition. Later legends refer to letters, manuscripts, and codices in the early Celtic church, particularly in connection with the communication with broader Christianity. Pryce argues that

> the origins of literacy in Wales are to be sought in the Romano-British Church which survived into the post-Roman period. Although pagan funerary and other inscriptions survive from certain Roman sites in Wales ... the Church was the institution which ensured that the written word, and the codex or book in particular, became a permanent, if for many a marginal, part of British and subsequently Welsh society. (Pryce, 1998: 3)

Literacy, manuscripts, and books were centered in the strongholds of the Church, particularly in the monastic communities, which expanded in

---

[10] Pryce, 1998: 3.

power and influence in the post-Roman British Isles, both in the Celtic kingdoms and in the newly emerging Anglo-Saxon kingdoms. As the monastic orders spread, they took with them Christian literacy, Christian manuscripts, and Christian codices.

The most significant of the monastic orders was the one centered at St. Davids, in Pembrokeshire. According to *Buchedd Dewi* ("Life of David"), the eleventh-century history written by Rhygyfarch, David was born around 500 CE near Henfynyw in Ceredigion. In a remarkable lifetime, David created a monastic order, presided over synods, founded churches and monasteries throughout Wales and Brittany, and was eventually named Bishop of Mynyw (now named St. Davids in his honor). Legend says that on one occasion, while David was preaching in Llanddewibrefi, the ground rose up beneath him to form a new hill, about which Davies writes, "in view of the nature of the landscape of Ceredigion, it would be difficult to conceive of any miracle more superfluous" (Davies, 2007a: 74).

Even with a "superfluous" miracle, David became the most important early Christian influence in Wales. The monastic order he founded, with an "emphasis on hard work, vegetarianism, and temperance" (Davies, 2007a: 73) was the model for other monastic orders throughout the Celtic fringe. David's monastery and later cathedral became a major center of monastic life and learning for the whole of the British Isles. In the late 800s, Alfred the Great recruited monks and gathered materials from St. Davids to promote education and literacy in the nation of Wessex. Centuries later, in 1081, William the Conqueror made a pilgrimage to the site a central part of his conquest west through the island. The cathedral there was considered so holy and important, in fact, that in 1123 Pope Calixtus II declared "Two pilgrimages to St Davids is equal to one to Rome, and three pilgrimages to one to Jerusalem" (St. Davids Cathedral's Famous Faces).

The centrality of St. Davids to British Christianity was based in the cult of St. David and in the importance of the manuscripts and relics it contained. It was seen as the home of spiritual and secular knowledge for the entire island. Unfortunately, St. Davids' collections also made it the target of raids and conquests by the Anglo-Saxons, the Vikings, and the Normans, and finally the successive destructions of the Dissolution of the Monasteries and the republican forces of Oliver Cromwell. Today, St. Davids remains recognized as one of the most important religious sites in Britain, although it is vastly diminished and its great Bishop's Palace lies in ruins.

St. Davids was at the center of British Christianity for centuries, with good reason. The Celtic Christianity practiced by the Romano-British at St. Davids and other monastic sites – with its associated literacy – became the major foundation of the churches in Scotland, Ireland, and the other parts of the Celtic fringe (Pryce, 1998: 3). Literacy was much more than a tool for communication; it was an essential component of Christianity, vital for preserving and spreading the word of God. Just as important, in the violent centuries that followed the fall of Rome, literacy and manuscripts were tangible connections to the Roman civilization that had been lost.

In Wales, early literacy was largely confined to the monasteries and to some of the ruling classes, and the focus was on religious texts. As noted above, the Welsh bards were the mainstay of preserving the histories, mythologies, and language of Wales. It wasn't until the 800s and even later that bardic epics, poems, and histories began to be written down and preserved in manuscripts.

3.3 Written Welsh

The Father has wrought [such a multitude] of wonders in this world
  That it is difficult to find an equal number
  Letters cannot contain it, letters cannot express it.
        —Anonymous Scribe in Juvencus, *Evangeliorum Libri*[11]

The inscribed stones that show early literacy in Wales eventually gave way to other written texts about Christianity. By the eighth and ninth centuries, there was a marked increase in the number of manuscripts and codices that were produced in Wales. Several developments contributed to this increased number of texts.

---

[11] The Juvencus Englynion.

First, monasteries in the British Isles began to transition from houses of austere living to centers of learning and knowledge. St. Davids led the way after the archbishopric of Caerleon was moved to St. Davids in 519 and the cathedral and monastic community became the most important center of learning for the entirety of Britain. Other monasteries patterned themselves after St. Davids and began producing and copying important Christian codices.

Second, in 768 Christians in Wales finally adopted the Roman Catholic Easter, which symbolized the end of Celtic Christianity as an independent church with its own rites. This Romanization of the Celtic churches meant the loss of traditional practices, but it also connected the churches and monasteries in Wales to each other and to churches throughout Britain. As Pryce states: "Paschal orthodoxy smoothed the way for greater contacts between the clergy in Wales and those in neighboring territories, especially the Anglo-Saxon kingdoms, with whom they had previously not been in communion, thereby providing channels for the transmission of books and ideas" (Pryce, 1998: 5). Letters, manuscripts, and books began to travel between the religious centers in Wales, the churches in the Anglo-Saxon kingdoms, and even the churches in continental Europe.

Third, political changes – the increased power of Welsh princes, the ongoing border struggles with the Anglo-Saxons, and the initial incursions by the Vikings – inspired new kinds of texts. Border disputes and inheritance struggles led to the codification of Welsh law, and resistance against their neighbors' expansion led to works of history that set Wales apart and established Welsh princely authority.

Based on these changes to Welsh society, from the mid-700s we begin to see an increasing number of texts produced in Wales, most in Latin, but a few in other languages, including, for the first time, Welsh. These texts and codices made their way to other libraries throughout Britain. Alfred the Great's library included a number of Latin manuscripts from Wales.

Two of the most important of these medieval books are *Historia Brittonum*, a history of Wales written in about 829 at the court of Gwynedd, and *Cyfraith Hywel*, written in the mid-920s in Seisyllwyg. *Historia Brittonum* is the earliest compiled history of Wales that brings together multiple sources, including "Bede, Anglo-Saxon genealogies and king-lists, Irish and Welsh hagiographical texts, northern British annals . . . a poem in Welsh cataloguing the battles of Arthur, and the story of the foundation of Gwynedd" (Pryce, 1998: 5). This history showed an effort to create a Welsh identity and to legitimize the authority of the Welsh rulers by connecting them to earlier heroes and Roman civilization.

Cyfraith Hywel, on the other hand, was created a century later to regulate the laws of the entire country. In 920, Hywel Dda was named the prince of Seisyllwyg. During the almost thirty years of his reign, Hywel gained control over most of Wales through marriage, alliance, and conquest – helped significantly by his close relationship with Alfred the Great's grandson Æthelstan, who was unifying England at the same time. More importantly, however, Hywel gathered a council of princes, clergy, and legal advisors to codify Welsh law for the entire country. This process was described in the introduction to *Cyfraith Hywel*:

> Hywel the Good, son of Cadell, king of Wales, was moved by the grace of God and fasting and prayer during his reign over Wales . . . There were bad customs and bad laws before his time. He therefore summoned six men from every cwmwd in Wales and brought them to the White House on the river Taf; and among them there were those who held croziers in Wales, including archbishops and bishops and abbots and good teachers; and also among those people, twelve of the wisest laymen were chosen, and the wisest scholar who was called Blegywyrd, to make good laws and to abolish the bad ones which existed before his time; and to replace them with good ones and to confirm them in his own name. (Newton, 2016)

Cyfraith Hywel, the first comprehensive set of Welsh laws, was sent to Rome to be approved and blessed by the Pope. These laws encompassed criminal laws, civil laws, and laws governing succession and inheritances, and served as the legal authority in Wales for six centuries until they were replaced by the Laws in Wales Acts of 1535–42. Most significantly, *Cyfraith*

Hywel was written in Welsh, representing a turn away from the Latin-based culture of the post-Roman period and a turn toward a uniquely Welsh literate culture.

In between *Historia Brittonum* and *Cyfraith Hywel* can be seen the emergence of Welsh writing. There are earlier examples of Welsh writing, of course, and there are certainly some samples that have been lost to time. But in the 800s and 900s, Welsh glosses and commentaries on Latin works begin to appear (Fulton, 2019: 28). These manuscripts show the decline of Latin and the rise of Welsh as the standard language of the elite and of the student class. As Pryce argues, "it was this decline in Latinity which provided the crucial stimulus to the development of written Welsh from the late eighth century onwards" (Pryce, 1998: 6).

Additionally, during this time the earliest written Welsh poetry appears as marginalia in Latin manuscripts. One Welsh scribe, copying Juvencus' *Evangeliorum Libri* sometime in the mid-900s, added twelve stanzas of poetry in the margins. In one stanza, he writes:

It cluis it humil inhared celmed	Purely, humbly, in skillful verse
Rit pucsaun mi detrintaut	I should give praise to the Trinity,
Gurd meint iconidid imolaut	According to the greatness of his power.

(The Juvencus Englynion)

This poetry is important for many reasons. First, it provides evidence of the Welsh language as the primary language of the scribes in the tenth century – Latin was the language of the Church and of books, but Welsh was the language of traditional poetry. Second, the twelve verses in the Juvencus manuscript are the earliest written examples of Welsh *Englynion*, a poetry form with rigid metre and rhyme patterns. That the scribe is writing this kind of poem as marginalia shows that the Englynion forms already existed and that he was likely capturing an oral poem composed by himself or a Welsh bard. Finally, these poems capture a rare glimpse into the life and thoughts of a monastic copyist as he produced religious manuscripts.

3.4 The Mabinogion

Be silent, then, ye unlucky rhyming bards,
For you cannot judge between truth and falsehood.
If you be primary bards formed by heaven,
Tell your king what his fate will be.
        —Taliesin, in *The Mabinogion*[12]

In the late 1830s, Lady Charlotte Guest, a British aristocrat and linguist, published a seven-volume set of medieval Welsh literature called the *Mabinogion*. Guest presented the collection as a cohesive set of Welsh legends that were not only important to the history of Wales and the British Isles, but were actually vital source texts for much of medieval European literature, including the chivalric stories surrounding King Arthur. In her introduction to the *Mabinogion*, Guest makes a detailed argument for it as a source text:

> It might, I think, be shown, by pursuing the inquiry, that the Cymric nation is not only, as Dr. Prichard has proved it to be, an early offshoot of the Indo-European family, and a people of unmixed descent, but that when driven out of their conquests by the later nations, the names and exploits of their heroes, and the compositions of their bards, spread far and wide among the invaders, and affected intimately their tastes and literature for many centuries, and that it has strong claims to be considered the cradle of European Romance. (Guest, 1877: xx)

Guest's books include Welsh and English versions of legends about the early rulers of Wales, including their travels, their struggles, their romances, and their deaths. The stories of Math fab Mathonwy, Gwydion, Pryderi, Branwen Ferh Llŷr, the bard Taliesin, and King Arthur that are included in the *Mabinogion* have influenced modern fantasy

---

[12] Guest, 1877: 485.

writers, including Evangeline Walton, who directly adapted the *Mabinogion* into a series of novels beginning in the 1930s; J. R. R. Tolkien, who based *The Silmarillion* (begun in 1914, but ultimately published posthumously in 1977) on the *Mabinogion*; Lloyd Alexander, whose Chronicles of Prydain (published in the 1960s) includes characters and story elements from the *Mabinogion*; and a number of books, television shows, and films that adapt the stories or draw from the themes of the ancient Welsh mythologies (Aronstein, 2019: 622–26).

Although Guest's version of the *Mabinogion* was hugely influential, it misrepresented the history of the Welsh stories it contained and overstated their connection with each other. In truth, the collection of Welsh myths now known as the *Mabinogion* represent eleven distinct legends. The most important of the legends are the complex Four Branches of the *Mabinogi*, which tell the stories of Pwyll Prince of Dyfed, Branwen Daughter of Llŷr, Manawydan Son of Llŷr, and Math Son of Mathonwy. These four stories weave together the history and magic of early medieval Wales which "presents a past where British kings ruled over the entire Island of Britain" (Luft, 2019: 82–3). The other stories in the collection include *The Dream of Macsen Wledig*, *Lludd and Llefelys*, *Culhwch and Olwen*, *The Dream of Rhonabwy*, and *The Tale of Taliesin*, along with *The Three Welsh Romances*, which are Arthurian legends that share features with Chrétien de Troyes's romanticized tales of King Arthur.

In the time since Guest's publication of her collection, her claims about the origins, connections, and influence have been the source of much scholarly debate. The earliest written manuscripts that include these texts appeared in the late 1300s with the *White Book of Rhydderch* in 1375 and the *Red Book of Hergest* in 1400. These manuscripts seem to be collections of earlier oral stories, with some references to the oral transmission of the tales in the documents themselves. But beyond that is a complex mystery. Luft sums up the current state of scholarly understanding of the origins of the *Mabinogion*:

> Despite more than a century of scholarship, there is little concrete information upon which to base an analysis of these tales. The basic facts of their composition – the who,

> when, where, or why – remain the subject of debate. We
> do not know who wrote the texts, or who read them (or
> listened to them read aloud) . . . We do not know with any
> certainty when or where the texts were produced.
>
> (Luft, 2019: 73)

Clues in the texts themselves point toward authorship dates in the
eleventh or twelfth centuries, and perhaps even earlier. Given the nature
of the stories and the fact that they contain elements of pre-Christian
Celtic mythologies combined with later Christian themes, there is the
possibility that the stories that evolved into the *Mabinogion* were present
in Welsh society for centuries before they were written down. On the
other hand, the dominant themes in the stories "of the loss of sovereignty of Britain and the hopes of its restoration under a prophesied
ruler" (Luft, 2019: 82) seem to connect to an origin after the Norman
invasion of Wales.

In spite of the uncertainty of the origins of the *Mabinogion*, the
importance of the collection to the history of Welsh publishing cannot
be overemphasized. First, the *Maginogion* is evidence of the transition
from an oral culture to a textual culture. The stories refer to their
performance by bards and contain elements of poetry and song that
can be connected to the sixth-century poetry of Aneirin and Taliesin
(Huws, 2008: 390). In addition, Sioned Davies argues that to fully
understand the *Mabinogion*, readers need to see them as written versions
of oral tales:

> Oral and performance features are an integral part of their
> fabric, partly because the authors inherited pre-literary
> modes of narrating, but also because the written tales were
> composed for oral delivery, so that their reception and
> dissemination continued to have an influence on both style
> and structure. (Davies, 2007b: 13)

Second, the *White Book* and the *Red Book* represent the bulk of original
Welsh-language prose in medieval manuscripts. While we have

examples of Welsh law and Welsh poetry, there are very few examples of Welsh prose (see Huws, 2008: 391–92). Part of this is due to the suppression of Welsh and the loss of the monastic libraries. But a larger part of this is due to the bardic traditions that kept oral storytelling as the primary form of transmission for the important Welsh stories, while written manuscripts and codices were secondary.

Third, the creation of the *White Book of Rhydderch* and the *Red Book of Hergest* shows a renewed interest in Welsh language and culture in the century after the Edwardian conquest of Wales. In the late 1300s, England's domination of Wales was wavering as it dealt with internal struggles. The emergence of written Welsh mythologies coincided with a rise in Welsh nationalism that culminated in the revolt of Owain Glyndŵr. Glyndŵr himself built his support by connecting his revolt and his position as Prince of Wales to Welsh mythology in the *Mabinogion* and the more extensive Arthurian legends. In fact, in 1403, when Glyndŵr was at Carmarthen, he summoned the patron of the *Red Book* to consult about history and to prophesy of his future reign (Luft, 2019: 84). As Luft argues, "Whatever the original purpose of these texts, it seems that by the fourteenth century they had been . . . turned into a narrative of the return of power to the Welsh" (Luft, 2019: 84).

Finally, the modern publication of the *Mabinogion* coincides with another Welsh revival in the eighteenth and nineteenth centuries. William Owen Pughe began the modern publications of the *Mabinogion* with English translations of individual stories starting in 1795 (Pughe, 1795). He was followed by Guest's more thorough and more influential editions of the *Mabinogion* in the 1830s and 1840s, with an English-only edition published in 1877. These volumes, which were "a testimony to a primitive, wild, lawless people, a curious tradition to be preserved and compared" (Aronstein, 2019: 622), sold in huge numbers throughout Wales, England, and the United States, and set the foundation for twentieth-century fantasy novels with their Celticized worlds (Aronstein, 2019: 623). This uniquely Welsh collection of legends has been hugely influential for centuries, both in Wales and in the larger publishing world.

3.5 King Arthur

Yet somme men say in many partyes of Englond that kyng Arthur is not deed
But had by the wylle of our lord Ihesu in to another place
and men say that he shal come ageyn & he shal wynne the holy crosse.
—Sir Thomas Malory, *Le Morte D'Arthur*[13]

The most important character to come out of medieval Welsh mythology is without a doubt King Arthur. Few other characters from world history have had as much effect on storytelling, publishing, and modern media. His legends have been published and republished; reworked and modernized; parodied and memorialized; and filmed and reimagined. This sixth-century Celtic hero has become the preeminent British king, and the inspiration for Romantic notions of medieval chivalry throughout Britain and Europe. He is celebrated throughout the British Isles and in English literature, even though it was the ancestors of the English people who Arthur was fighting against. As an historical and mythological character, Arthur is formidable; as the subject of publishing, Arthur has provided centuries of profitable material.

The earliest Arthurian myths place Arthur in Wales as the leader of a united group of Britons who fought against the invading Anglo-Saxons. The *Historia Brittonum* (written around 828 CE) reports that in the Battle of Badon in roughly 516 CE, Arthur led the charge and killed 960 Anglo-Saxon soldiers, "and no one struck them down except Arthur himself" (Nennius, 1848). These early writings don't necessarily refer to Arthur as a king; rather, he seemed to be a mighty warrior and perhaps a warlord. The designation of Arthur as a king came in later sources, including *Culhwch ac Olwen* (later included in the *Mabinogion*), which is "the earliest vernacular account of Arthur's leadership" (Luft, 2019: 84; see also Bromwich & Evans, 2012), and Geoffrey of Monmouth's *Historia Regum Brittaniae* – a largely invented history of Britain written in 1136 and based in part on *Historia Brittonum*.

Whether Arthur actually existed as an individual, a soldier, a king, or as a combination of several historical figures has been debated for centuries. The answer, if there is one, is lost to time and layers of legend and myth. But

---

[13] Malory, 1889: 851.

the Arthurian legends mark the ideal point of post-Roman Britain, where the enlightened Christian Britons were unified in fighting a holy battle against the invading heathen armies of the Anglo-Saxons. In the legend, the Britons were only defeated when they beat themselves, through treachery, infighting, and individual unworthiness. Arthur's death at the Battle of Camlann in ca. 537 CE brought about a dissolution of the Kingdom of the Britons into several smaller and weaker kingdoms.

Arthur's might in battle, supernatural associations, and divinely appointed kingship, along with the stories of his Knights of the Round Table, were added in medieval retellings of the legends. *Historia Regum Brittaniae*, originally written in Latin, was translated and distributed throughout Britain and Europe, and later writers expanded the tales and combined them with their own mythologies. Chrétien de Troyes, writing in France in the late 1100s, added stories about Lancelot, Percival, and the search for the Holy Grail, the details of which were highly influenced by the society, ideals, and saints of medieval France. The Celtic hero became an idealized French king, and thus became the model for the Norman kings of England, as well as kings throughout Europe.

In the history of Wales, connecting one's rule to King Arthur seemed to be an essential element of claiming supremacy and calling for unity. Llewelyn the Great patterned his rule after Arthur's, and stories about Llewelyn echo Arthurian myth: He united Wales against a foreign foe; he ruled over a powerful court of princes and knights; he grew in power enough to end the wars with the English and usher in a golden age where he reigned in peace. Unfortunately, Llywelyn also shared some of the darker elements of Arthurian myth. His wife, Joan, was caught having an affair with William de Braose, Lord of Abergavenny, which broke the hard-won peace and raised questions of the legitimacy of his successors. And, like Arthur, Llywelyn's power was based on his own personality and his relationship with England, rather than on an enduring dynasty. As historian David Moore wrote:

> When Llywelyn died in 1240 his principatus of Wales rested
> on shaky foundations. Although he had dominated Wales,
> exacted unprecedented submissions and raised the status of

the prince of Gwynedd to new heights, his three major
ambitions – a permanent hegemony, its recognition by the
king, and its inheritance in its entirety by his heir – remained
unfulfilled. His supremacy, like that of Gruffydd ap
Llywelyn, had been merely personal in nature, and there
was no institutional framework to maintain it either during
his lifetime or after his death. (Moore, 2005: 126)

Later in the same century, the English king Edward I also emphasized
his ties to Arthurian legend. The castles that he built in Wales and the
structures of government he introduced were explicitly tied to the stories
about Arthur that were being reimported to England and Wales from
France. In suppressing the Welsh revolt, Edward claimed that he was
acting in the role of Arthur to unify and civilize Britain under a chivalric
order. Norman historian Peter Langtoft, a contemporary of Edward I,
wrote:

Of chivalry, after king Arthur,
Was king Edward the flower of Christendom.
He was so handsome and great, so powerful in arms,
That of him may one speak as long as the world lasts.
For he had no equal as a knight in armour
For vigour and valour, neither present nor future.
(Douglas & Rothwell, 2006: 256)

A century after Edward I claimed Wales and Arthur for England, the
Welsh Prince Owain Glyndŵr reclaimed the legend for himself. In most
accounts of his revolt, Glyndŵr presents himself as a return to the
glorious reign of Arthur, and sometimes as the prophesied return of
Arthur himself. Glyndŵr based his troop movements, his government,
and his proposal to divide up the island of Britain on stories of Arthur
and Merlin. To the English, this came across as being superstitious and
more than a little egocentric. Writing two centuries later, William
Shakespeare had Owain describe himself in glowing, supernatural
terms:

Give me leave
To tell you once again that at my birth
The front of heaven was full of fiery shapes,
The goats ran from the mountains, and the herds
Were strangely clamorous to the frighted fields.
These signs have mark'd me extraordinary;
And all the courses of my life do show
I am not in the roll of common men.

                                   (*Henry IV*, Act 3, Scene 1)

To the Welsh, however, Owain Glyndŵr was a hero. He fought against the English and won back most of Wales, even though he had fewer soldiers and fewer resources than the English king. He became a symbol of Welsh nationalism and a mythic character who could rival King Arthur in his own right. It only helped build his legend when Glyndŵr's end was shrouded in mist; rather than dying in battle, Glyndŵr simply disappeared into the foggy Welsh hills. Like Arthur, Glyndŵr is said to be waiting to return and lead the Welsh to a glorious new golden age of independence.

Chrétien's epic Arthurian poems were expanded by unknown authors in France; they were also connected in some way to the Arthurian sections of the *Mabinogion*, although scholars are uncertain whether Chrétien inspired the *Mabinogion* or if they shared some undiscovered written or oral source about Arthur.

All of these sources contributed to the most influential Arthurian work: *Le Morte D'Arthur*, by Sir Thomas Malory. The identity of Malory is in doubt, but the most likely candidate is a fifteenth-century nobleman who led a life distinctly at odds with the chivalric ideals he wrote about (Whitteridge, 1973). Malory was imprisoned for theft, kidnapping, rape, and possibly attempted murder. It was during one of his times in prison that he compiled *Le Morte D'Arthur*, based heavily on greatly embellished continental sources rather than the older English and Welsh Arthurian tales. Malory called his work *The Hoole Book of Kyng Arthur and of His Noble Knyghtes of The Rounde Table*. When it was published by William Caxton in 1495, however, Caxton changed the title to *Le Morte D'Arthur* and created what has become the definitive Arthurian source for centuries.

Arthurian legend, which was incredibly popular in handwritten medieval manuscripts, has been a rich source of material for publishing since the advent of printing. In addition to centuries of editions and translations of *Le Morte D'Arthur*, King Arthur's stories have inspired hundreds of novels, poetic works, plays, pieces of music, films, and television shows in dozens of languages. Of all of the Welsh contributions to modern publishing, Arthur – the Celtic warlord transformed into an enduring chivalric icon – stands above the rest.

3.6 Gerald of Wales

I have thought good to commit to writing the devout visitation which Baldwin, archbishop of Canterbury, made throughout Wales; and to hand down, as it were in a mirror, through you, O illustrious Stephen, to posterity, the difficult places through which we passed, the names of springs and torrents, the witty sayings, the toils and incidents of the journey, the memorable events of ancient and modern times, and the natural history and description of the country; lest my study should perish through idleness, or the praise of these things be lost by silence.

—Gerald of Wales[14]

Gerald was a prominent Norman-Welsh priest born in Pembrokeshire in the mid-1100s. He had ties by blood or service to the great families of Wales, Ireland, and England. In 1176, he was even nominated to be the bishop of St. Davids, but his candidacy was rejected by King Henry II, who was afraid that having a Welsh bishop in St. Davids would be a challenge to his own power. Instead, the king appointed Gerald to be a royal clerk and chaplain, as well as a liaison to the powerful Welsh Prince Rhys ap Gruffydd.

Gerald's duties to the royal house included traveling through the territories ruled by Henry II – first Ireland, with Henry's son John (the same John who later became king, signed the Magna Carta, and was memorialized as the

---

[14] Gerald, 1997:b.

villain of the Robin Hood legends), and then Wales, with the Archbishop of Canterbury. Gerald wrote detailed accounts of his journeys that are valuable records of the history, culture, and attitudes of the twelfth-century British Isles. His trip through Ireland in 1185 resulted in two books: *Topographia Hibernica* ("Topography of Ireland") and *Expugnatio Hibernica* ("Conquest of Ireland"), both of which appeared in roughly 1188. These two books were widely copied throughout the medieval period and were printed in multiple editions in the early days of print.

Gerald's observations about Ireland and its people were harsh:

> But although they are richly endowed with the gifts of nature, their want of civilisation, shown both in their dress and mental culture makes them a barbarous people . . .
>
> The Irish are a rude people, subsisting on the produce of their cattle only, and living themselves like beasts . . .
>
> They neither employ themselves in the manufacture of flax or wool or in any kind of trade or mechanical art; but abandoning themselves to idleness, and immersed, in sloth, their greatest delight is to be exempt from toil, their richest possession, the enjoyment of liberty. (Wright, 1863)

Gerald's comments about the Irish likely reflected Norman biases against the Irish Celts rather than actual observations (there is some evidence that Gerald's travels in Ireland were fairly limited). Even so, his books were widely circulated and remained the dominating narrative about the Irish through the seventeenth and eighteenth centuries. Indeed, similar language can be seen in anti-Irish publications of the nineteenth and twentieth centuries, both in the United Kingdom and the United States.

In 1188, just as he was finishing his *Topographia Hibernica*, Gerald was chosen to travel with the Archbishop of Canterbury on a tour through Wales in order to drum up support for the Third Crusade. Henry II needed the support of the powerful Welsh princes and the Marcher lords to carry out his crusade, and Gerald, with his ties to both Welsh and Norman nobility, was an ideal man to help make the argument. Unlike Gerald's tour of Ireland, which was less than thorough, his travel through Wales was extensive. While the immediate impetus for the tour was the Third Crusade, Gerald's writings about Wales reveal that he was addressing a larger problem for the king: What to do with Wales?

The 1188 journey resulted in two books which provide important details about medieval Wales: *Itinerarium Cambriae* ("Itinerary through Wales") in 1191 and *Descriptio Cambriae* ("Description of Wales") in 1194. These books offered Gerald's observations of Wales, its people, and the Welsh language, but they also provided advice for the English rulers on how to conquer and maintain control over Wales. This advice included recommendations to divide the Welsh princes, subdue Welsh language and culture, and to use the knowledge of the Marcher lords (many of whom, like Gerald, had both Norman and Welsh ancestry) to the advantage of the English.

Even though the books were written with the intent to help the English king subdue the Welsh, Gerald maintains a much more even tone in these volumes than he does in his *Hibernica* volumes. Perhaps because of his own ancestry and personal connections to the Welsh, or because he conducted more personal observations in Wales than he did in Ireland, *Itinerarium Cambriae* and *Descriptio Cambriae* contain balanced descriptions that remain incredibly useful as sources of information about medieval Wales.

Although these four works are the most influential books that Gerald wrote, he also contributed at least seventeen other books of history, geography, and religion to medieval libraries, including detailed biographies of St. David and St. Ethelbert. Gerald's major works are still published and studied, in both print and digital forms.

3.7 The Dissolution of the Monasteries

Be it enacted, by authority of this present Parliament, that the king, our sovereign lord, his heirs and successors, kings of this realm, shall be taken, accepted, and reputed the only supreme head in earth of the Church of England, called Anglicana Ecclesia.

—Act of Supremacy, 1534[15]

[15] Ross, n.d.

The Tudor era was marked with increased oppression of Welsh language and culture, but it also was the beginning of a renaissance for Welsh arts and industry. The end to the border conflicts and the integration of the Marcher lordships into the English county system led to a time of relative peace and prosperity. Additionally, the Tudor policies toward Wales led to a resurgence of interest in traditional Welsh culture and the development of new industries. In 1523, for the first time in almost 400 years, a large-scale *eisteddfod* was held in Caerwys. This revival of the ancient bardic festival was a recognition of the Tudor Welsh heritage and the desired unification of the two countries. In 1567, Elizabeth I became the first English monarch to sponsor an eisteddfod.

But Tudor-era reforms also struck a huge blow against the preserved history of the British Isles. The 1534 Act of Supremacy that established Henry VIII as the head of the Church of England also gave him possession of all Church properties, declaring that he should

> have and enjoy, annexed and united to the imperial crown of
> this realm, as well the title and style thereof, as all honors,
> dignities, preeminences, jurisdictions, privileges, authori-
> ties, immunities, profits, and commodities to the said dignity
> of the supreme head of the same Church belonging and
> appertaining. (Ross, n.d.)

In practice, this meant that all of the lands, wealth, and libraries of the monasteries were transferred to the king. This was not a uniquely English event; monasteries throughout Europe had been seized by monarchs for their wealth or their perceived faults (or, more accurately, for their wealth *justified by* their perceived faults). But it was more widespread and more destructive in the British Isles, where the monarch had become the head of the Church. Nearly 900 religious houses were seized, involving almost 12,000 monks, nuns, canons, and friars (Bernard, 2011: 390). From the initial Dissolution in the late 1530s through the more violent purges of Edward VI and Mary, most of the religious houses in the British Isles were destroyed and their treasures seized, scattered, or burned. Forty-six of those monasteries were in Wales, and their relics and libraries were almost completely destroyed.

The monasteries of England and Wales had been storehouses of knowledge and priceless, irreplaceable manuscripts for nearly a thousand years before Henry VIII's reforms. These monastic libraries were destroyed; many of the libraries were able to preserve less than one percent of their holdings (Huws, 1998: 26). Additional purges of "dangerous" works took place under Edward VI, who confiscated and destroyed Catholic texts, and Mary, who did the same to Protestant works.

Scholars and Church officials recognized the huge loss that these books represented. In England, there was a concerted effort to preserve important books: John Leland was commissioned to collect books for King Henry's royal libraries; Archbishop of Canterbury Matthew Parker created his own large private collection, which he donated to Cambridge on his death; and Sir Thomas Bodley collected volumes later in the sixteenth century for the library at Oxford. In Wales, however, there were fewer efforts to collect and preserve the monastic libraries. Many of the Welsh manuscripts and books that were spared during the Dissolution did so because they were already at other monasteries. Only a handful of books that were in Welsh monastic libraries have survived to the present. Huws notes, "Whereas fifteen medieval libraries in England are each represented by over a hundred surviving books, only one Welsh library, that of Llanthony Prima, is represented by more than four" (Huws, 1998: 26).

Unfortunately, although we have some descriptions of the volumes in the monastic libraries of Wales, there is no complete catalogue. Again from Huws: "Of 242 titles listed at the rich Cisternian abbey of Margam in the early fourteenth century not one book is known to survive" (Huws, 1998: 26). We will never know just how many records were lost when the monasteries were destroyed. What we do know is that in the first 150 years after the invention of the printing press, many of the handwritten manuscripts that preserved the history, culture, and language of medieval Wales were lost forever.

3.8 Manuscripts and Printed Books

Letters are signs of things, symbols of words, whose power is so great that
without a voice they speak to us the words of the absent; for they introduce
words by the eye, not by the ear.

—Isidore of Seville[16]

The invention of printing (or, at least, Gutenberg's version of printing) began a new era for books. Printed books shared a physical form with their manuscript forebears and, at least in the first hundred years or so, were designed to have the appearance of carefully crafted manuscript books. Typefaces were created to emulate handwriting, and the compositors left spaces in the texts for illuminations and illustrations that were added later by hand. Even the materials used – gatherings of vellum or linen paper with leather- or cloth-covered wooden board covers – were largely the same.

The evolution from manuscript books to printed books involved much larger changes to literacy and society, however. Even within the same codex form, manuscripts and printed books were designed to be used differently. Manuscript books, because of the time and expense required for production, were never intended for wide distribution. They were created for individual clients with deep pockets: cathedrals, monasteries, royalty and nobility, and the rising merchant class. They were shared with larger audiences through public readings or performances, connecting them with the long history of oral storytelling. The books were tools to facilitate performances, rather than texts to be read individually.

Printed books, on the other hand, were designed for a wider distribution. Although Gutenberg's first clients were the same wealthy organizations and individuals who bought manuscript books, printing very quickly made texts available to a larger population. "For the first time, near-identical copies of texts were being produced in quantities limited only by economic expediency and distributed to a readership which was larger than a social community" (Evans, 2019: 213). Religious books, classical works, volumes of history and mythology, and poetry and song could be printed

---

[16] Brehaut, 1912: 96.

and distributed widely, breaking the boundaries of traditional nations and communities. Within the first hundred years of printing, millions of books were printed, flooding the market with all kinds of texts.

The new availability of books changed many things in society. Literacy, which was already on the rise in Europe, increased at a much faster pace. More importantly, the way people experienced texts changed. Rather than encountering texts through a social gathering where a single reader would perform the work, people began to read books individually and silently, and that soon became the primary way individuals experienced texts. The implications of these changes were (1) a greater shift from orality to literacy based on the greater availability and variety of texts; (2) an increased focus on individuality over community, leading to new ideas about the roles of monarchies, governments, churches, and individuals in society; (3) a change in the relationship between individuals and God, religion, science, philosophy, and other ideas, where individuals could explore and experience all of the big ideas of society without the mediating voice of a priest or a scholar. Overall, the move from manuscripts to print accompanied a larger shift in society that drove the Protestant Reformation, the Scientific Revolution, and the Enlightenment.

4 Early Welsh Printing

It is a press, certainly, but a press from which shall flow in inexhaustible
streams . . . A spring of truth shall flow from it: like a new star it shall scatter
the darkness of ignorance, and cause a light heretofore unknown to shine
amongst men.

—attributed to Johannes Gutenberg[17]

By the time of the Dissolution of the Monasteries, the printing press had
been around for nearly 100 years in Europe. Johannes Gutenberg's press
spread quickly through the continent and arrived in England with William
Caxton in 1476. The printing press jump-started the nascent Renaissance,
which brought with it a rediscovered interest in classical Greek and Latin
literature, language, and culture. But the printing press also opened the
doors to books, learning, and languages outside the classical canon.
Throughout Europe, printers began printing books, pamphlets, and other
materials in local vernaculars. There began to be a huge market for
translated materials, including classical texts, religious writings, political
and philosophical treatises, and local histories, myths, and stories.

In England, Caxton's press churned out English translations along with
Latin works. In all, Caxton himself printed over 100 books in just fifteen
years, a remarkable feat considering that printing was still a laborious
process, and a single book could take more than a year to produce. Many
of Caxton's translations became standards of English publishing, including
Le Morte D'Arthur and *Aesop's Fables,* and Caxton's version of printed
English became the basis for "correct" English.

Caxton's successor, Wynkyn de Worde, moved the press from
Westminster to Fleet Street in London, which quickly became the center
of British publishing, and remained so for centuries. Worde, in spite of
increasing government regulation of the press, increased the rate of book
production and laid the foundation for British presses to churn out

---

[17] De Lamartine, 1854: 334. Disclaimer: I have some doubts about the authenticity
of this quote. Its content seems more like a nineteenth-century invention than an
actual statement from Gutenberg.

hundreds of thousands of books by the end of the 1500s. This level of printed output in local languages was repeated throughout Europe. In the first hundred years of printing, thousands of translations were published for the first time.

But not in Wales. Welsh publishing, whether we take that to mean printing in the country or printing in the Welsh language, lagged significantly behind England and the rest of Europe. This is not because the Welsh were not aware of Gutenberg's invention. In 1480, only three years after Caxton printed his first book in England, the Welsh poet Bedo Brwynllys included references to the printing press at Westminster in a love poem (Evans, 2019: 212). Even with this awareness, the arrival of printing for the Welsh people took much longer. Much of this delay has to do with the restrictions that were place on Wales and Welsh during the early days of the printing press. Henry VIII's heavy hand prevented books from being translated into Welsh or printed in Wales. The result was that while hundreds of thousands of books were being printed throughout Europe and England in the 1500s, only thirty Welsh books were printed in the entire sixteenth century (Williams, 1998: 49).

This didn't mean that there weren't efforts to begin Welsh printing, of course. From the earliest days of printing, Welsh authors, Welsh religious leaders, and Welsh-language advocates began to push for books and other materials in Welsh. These pushes had to overcome several obstacles: the restrictive printing environment in England, the unfamiliarity with the Welsh language generally, and the broader cultural and religious clashes of the fifteenth and sixteenth centuries. This part of the story begins with the explosion of printing in the late fifteenth and early sixteenth centuries and the efforts by European monarchs to limit and control the new technology.

4.1 Restricting the Press

Besides we will grant, ordain, and appoint, for ourselves and the successors of us the foresaid Queen that no person within this our realm of England or the dominions of the same shall practice or exercise ... the art or mistery of printing any book ... unless the same person at the time of his foresaid printing is or shall be one of the community of the foresaid mistery or art of Stationery.

—Stationers' Charter, 1557[18]

When Johannes Gutenberg built his printing press in about 1450, he began a revolution in printing throughout Europe. Gutenberg's design for his press, moveable type, and other innovations spread through Europe and became a major player in the Renaissance and, later, in the Protestant Reformation. One of the advantages of the press (and one of the primary reasons it was opposed in many areas) is that it made religion and literature available to the common person, often in vernacular languages. For monarchs and religious leaders, the press represented a blessing and a curse. They recognized that the press had power to teach, educate, and convert people. But they also realized quickly that the press also had the power to influence or manipulate public opinion, create action, and foment rebellion.

For the first several decades after the first press was built, presses sprung up around Europe and had little or no regulation on what they printed, except for the limitations of money and time. Although printing was faster than the hand-copied manuscripts that preceded it, it was still prohibitively expensive – in both materials and labor – to run a press. Some of this cost was absorbed by consumers, who were eager to experience new books, particularly those in their own languages rather than Latin. But setting up a printing shop required resources, and most of the early printers had wealthy patrons or institutional clients (such as the Church or the government) or, in most cases, a combination of patrons and clients.

The expense of running presses and the patronage system initially kept the revolutionary new technology in check. After all, if the Bishop is funding the press, the Bishop has significant sway over what is published on that press. But as the popularity of the printed word grew, the patronage system fell apart, and printers in most places had extraordinary freedom to print whatever materials the market would buy. In many cases, this meant religious and political materials that were at odds with the traditional ruling powers.

---

[18] Arber, 1875: xxviii.

As the Protestant Reformation began in the 1500s, the power of the printing press came to the forefront. Martin Luther was particularly adept at using the press to spread his vision for church reform; he authored thousands of pamphlets that were printed, translated, and distributed throughout Europe. In response, the Church authorized and printed its own materials, creating a war of the printed word. Even King Henry VIII got involved, authoring the pamphlet *Assertio septem sacramentorum adversus Martinum Lutherum* ("Declaration of the Seven Sacraments Against Martin Luther"), which earned him the title "Defender of the Faith" from Pope Leo X.

Monarchs viewed the growing power of the press with alarm. The Church, which had been a traditional partner in maintaining the power of the crown, was splintering because of the rapid spread of Reformation literature. Kings who had derived their authority from the Church had to establish their own authority and combat the rising tides of anti-authoritarian sentiment. Henry VIII did this by reforming the laws of England, uniting the kingdoms of England and Wales, splitting from the Roman Church, and conducting a fairly brutal purge of those who opposed him. In the sixteenth and seventeenth centuries, English and European monarchs continued the trend of expanding their power and cracking down on political or religious opposition. All too often, cracking down on opposition meant limiting the power of the press and destroying unfavorable literature. In England, the Dissolution of the Monasteries was as much about controlling information as it was about seizing lucrative Church properties.

The destruction of the monastic libraries was matched by an increased control over the production of books. William Caxton's press had significant freedom in the late 1400s in England. As the only working press in the British Isles, it could be used to print all of Caxton's translations as well as materials from European sources. Under Henry VIII, laws were enacted to protect the British market from European competitors, including a 1534 law that made it illegal to import bound books. This protected London's bookbinders and allowed for some censorship of the imported materials (Roberts, 2002: 144).

As the printing business quickly expanded to several operating presses by 1500, it began to encroach on the business of manuscript production, which had been officially controlled by London's Guild of Stationers since at least 1403. (If you tour Stationers' Hall in London, your guide will likely claim that the guild is at least a few hundred years older than that.) The desire to regulate the industry, control the flow of information, navigate the religious disputes in England, and stem the tide of dangerous texts flowing from Europe led Queen Mary I to grant a charter to the Stationers' Company in 1557. In part, this charter read:

> Besides we will grant, ordain, and appoint, for ourselves and the successors of us the foresaid Queen that no person within this our realm of England or the dominions of the same shall practice or exercise by himself or by his ministers, his servants or by any other person the art or mistery of printing any book or any thing or sale or traffic within this our realm of England or the dominions of the same, unless the same person at the time of his foresaid printing is or shall be one of the community of the foresaid mistery or art of Stationery of the foresaid City, or has therefore licence of us, or the heirs or successors of us the foresaid Queen by the letters patent of us or the heirs or successors of us the foresaid Queen. (Arber, 1875: xxviii)

This charter granted the Stationers the exclusive right to the printing press for all of England and Wales. It also gave them the right to seize and destroy any materials that were printed or copied without their approval. This exclusive right served the interests of both the monarchy and the Stationers. As Clair argues, "While the Stationers saw in the charter a means of protecting their craft from unregulated competition, the Crown saw in it a means of controlling the increasingly powerful printing press from which came so many seditions and heretical books" (Clair, 1976: 269). Gutenberg's vision of "a press from which shall flow in inexhaustible streams" (De Lamartine, 1854: 334) was curtailed by increasingly restrictive measures taken to protect the monarchy and the Church.

Even though Wales ceased to be a separate nation from England politically after Henry VIII's annexation of Welsh territories, the country was still distinct in religion, culture, and language. The restriction of printing to the Stationers in London left the Welsh with only three options for printing Welsh-language materials: (1) printing with the Stationers in England, (2) printing in Europe, or (3) printing illegally. Even with only a few books printed in Welsh in the sixteenth and seventeenth centuries, we have significant evidence that Welsh publishers worked with all three options.

4.2 Printing in England

And for to passe the tyme thys boook shal be plesaunte to rede in.
—William Caxton, preface to *Le Morte D'Arthur*[19]

As the printing industry expanded in the early sixteenth century, there began to be a desire to publish books to serve the Welsh market. Wealthy Welsh gentry and clergy pushed for materials to be printed in the Welsh language. There were several obstacles to printing in Welsh, however. First, as discussed earlier in the text, printing was officially restricted to the Stationers in London and Cambridge, and those presses were already busy with printing books in Latin, English, and French for the growing literate population of England.

Second, the Stationers were actively policing not just where things were printed, but the kind of things that were printed. Catholic and other noncomformist books were prevented from being printed, even if there were a large market for them. Books that were produced without the Stationers' approval could be seized and destroyed, and the people who produced the books could be fined or imprisoned.

Third, Welsh was a difficult language for printers. Most of the early printers, including William Caxton and Wynkyn de Worde, were either born or trained in Europe to print using the Latin characters that were standard on the continent. Characters and languages outside of the European standard required either transcription, respelling, or the creation of custom typefaces. Caxton faced this problem as he translated works into

---

[19] Malory, 1889.

English; the limitations of his imported European typefaces signaled the death knell for already struggling Anglo-Saxon letters in the alphabet. Welsh was even more challenging than English, with additional unique letters and digraphs not present in standard European typefaces.

In addition to the difficulty of the Welsh alphabet, the Welsh language itself was challenging for printers (and, for that matter, many of the people who lived in Wales). Printers, who relied on their own knowledge of languages, were baffled by the strange, ancient Welsh language. To get things printed accurately, Welsh authors or translators had to travel to the print offices and oversee compositing and proofreading in person. As Williams notes, "having to employ compositors who knew little or no Welsh, and being obliged to spend long spells in London to see their books through to publication, 'owing to the Welsh language being so hard and unusual a language to set for the press,' added hugely to the cost of printing and to the number of printer's errors" (Williams, 1998: 48).

In spite of these obstacles, Welsh books began to be printed in the mid-sixteenth century. In 1546 Sir John Price, a Welsh scholar and medieval manuscript collector, published *Yny lhyvyr hwnn* ("In This Book"). This volume, printed in London, offered Price's thoughts on religion and morality and included a Welsh alphabet and reading guide as well as Welsh translations of the Lord's Prayer, Creed, and the Ten Commandments. As the earliest Welsh-language printed book, *Yny lhyvyr hwnn* is important. But even more so, the book shows that the themes that dominated Welsh published for centuries – religion and the preservation of the Welsh language – were there from the beginning of Welsh printing. The National Library of Wales holds the only known surviving copy of this book (Price, 1546).

Shortly after the publication of *Yny lhyvyr hwnn*, there began to be a push to publish the Bible in Welsh. The Protestant Reformation had opened the door for the Bible to be printed in local languages throughout Europe. In Wales, the advance of literacy and the difficulties of the transition from Catholicism to the new Anglican Communion led Church officials to begin the translation process. In particular, Anglican officials believed that a Welsh Bible would help convince some of the Catholic holdouts to conform with the state religion.

The primary difficulty with the desire for a Welsh Bible was Welsh itself. It presented both legal and linguistic barriers for the people who hoped to translate the holy book. Legally, English was the only official language of the United Kingdom, and it was the only language that could be used for any official publications. With the monarch being the head of the Anglican Church, Church publications, including the Bible, were restricted by the English-only law.

These restrictions on Welsh were official, but they were also becoming culturally significant. Just as the power of the printing press made a specific version of London English standard, the lack of printed Welsh materials, whether religious or secular, had a chilling effect on the desire of Welsh citizens to learn, speak, or read their native tongue.

Nevertheless, William Salesbury began a Welsh translation of portions of the New Testament, which he published in 1551. This was followed by translations of other religious pamphlets and materials, including the Book of Common Prayer. Finally, in 1563, an Act of Parliament authorized the translation of the entire Bible into Welsh. This monumental task was undertaken by Salesbury, Thomas Huet, and Richard Davies, Bishop of St. Davids. They published the New Testament in 1567.

In the 1570s, William Morgan, the vicar of Llanrhaeadr-ym-Mochnant, began his own translation of the Bible, including a revision of Salesbury's New Testament. Morgan explained his motivation for this translation in the introduction to his Bible when it was printed in 1588:

> When therefore I saw that the translation of the rest of the Scriptures was so useful, nay so necessary (though long deterred by the sense of my weakness, and the magnitude of the work, as well as the evil disposition of certain people) yielding to the wishes of the pious, I allowed myself to be persuaded to undertake this most important, troublesome and to many, unacceptable task.
>
> (Morgan, 1588)

The Welsh Bible was further revised by Bishop Richard Parry in the early 1600s, using the text of the newly published King James Bible. The Parry translation, published in 1620, is still the standard Welsh translation of the Bible, although there have been updates and new translations.

All of these translations of the Bible were printed in London, under the careful watch of Welsh speakers who checked the compositors' work. This same process was used on the other Welsh books that were published during this time. The difficulty of translation, composition, and printing meant that only a tiny number of books were printed in Welsh during the sixteenth and seventeenth centuries.

The Welsh market for printed books was growing, however, and in 1585 the printer Joseph Barnes was allowed to set up a press at Oxford. One of Barnes' goals for this press was to supply the Welsh market with books (Gruffydd, 1998: 61). As has always been the case with the Welsh book market, the majority of the books printed in Oxford were in English or Latin, which, along with French, were the preferred languages of the educated class. But the press at Oxford also printed Welsh materials, particularly smaller religious works.

Although printing in England presented challenges for Welsh authors and translators, it proved to be vitally important in the history of Wales. The publication of the Welsh Bible and other official Church documents ensured the survival of the Welsh language, not just as a curious vernacular, but as the native language of Wales. Although Welsh was still officially suppressed in government, legal documents, and the courts, the fact that it could be used in liturgical settings made it socially acceptable, both for the general public and the elite.

In general, however, the printing of Welsh-language materials lagged far behind the English-language counterparts, and although "a few Welsh books would be printed in Oxford and a small number of recusant texts were printed in France and Italy" (Evans, 2019: 215), London's print shops (with all of their restrictions) were the center of Welsh publishing efforts. One effect of this was that "it also helped to preserve the culture of manuscript production in Wales, a culture which was the dominant form for the preservation and transmission of written texts well into the sixteenth century and was still an active part of Welsh literary life ... [in the] eighteenth century" (Evans, 2019: 2015). Without presses at home, and with challenges in printing in England or abroad, the Welsh kept producing manuscripts much later than the rest of England and Europe.

The publishing industry in England continued to expand and, after Parliament lifted restrictions on printing locations in 1660, presses were established in several locations. Presses in England continued to serve Wales until there was a ring of printers and booksellers surrounding the small country. The two most important areas for Welsh publishing after 1660 were Shrewsbury and Chester, which produced more popular works in contrast to the "scholarly and subsidized philanthropic works" produced in London and Oxford (Rees, 1998: 123). Even after presses began to be established in Wales in the 1700s, the majority of printed books came from the publishing centers in England.

4.3 Printing in Europe

> *Every country, by the grace and favour of the Triune God,*
> *Has begun to print in towns:*
> *Through the exercise of virtue it would be no harder*
> *If the same work were done in our language.*
> —Sir Lewis Gethin, 1529[20]

European printing was several decades ahead of the printing industry in England. While William Caxton set up his press in Westminster only twenty-six years after Gutenberg debuted the printing press in Mainz, by that time there were roughly seventy presses operating in Germany and Italy (Clair, 1976: 94), and more being established in France, Belgium, and other locations throughout the continent.

Caxton's press was unusual because it was the only one outside of Germany where "the pioneer of the new art was a native of the country" (Clair, 1976: 94). Most printers were trained at one of the older presses in Germany or France and then went to establish their own presses in new areas. As new presses were established in England to compete with Caxton, their owners came from all over Europe: Theodore Rood, from Cologne; Johannes Lettou, from

[20] Gruffydd, 1998: 55.

Lithuania; William de Machlinia, from Flanders; and Caxton's foreman and successor, Wynkyn de Worde, from Lorraine (Clair, 1976: 97–100).

The backgrounds of the printers in England are important for two reasons. First, very few of the printers in England were printing in their own native language. They printed books in Latin, French, English, and eventually Welsh (among a few other languages). While Caxton himself could use his knowledge of English in producing his translations, his successors were often translating from one foreign tongue to another (this makes it all the more remarkable to see the quality of the English in those early books). Welsh was difficult, but it was simply another foreign language, especially once Latin transcriptions of Welsh letters and sounds were established.

Second, the printers in England had extensive contact with the printers in Europe. It was a small trade, and most of the early printers had interacted with each other, either through their training, through competition, or through bookselling partnerships. Booksellers were attached to print shops, and they often carried the works of printers from other printers within England or from continental Europe. By the end of the fifteenth century, England's printers were seeing competition from printers in France, Italy, and Belgium, who were all printing books for the English market (Clair, 1976: 106).

Reforms under the Tudor monarchs, including the charter of the Stationers and restrictions on the employment of foreigners, eliminated most of the foreign competition within England. The unintended effect, however, was that printers who wanted to operate outside of the Stationers' control left England for more open markets in Europe or Edinburgh. These printers included political dissidents, Catholics, and even those who just didn't want to go through the rigorous steps to qualify for acceptance into the Stationers. This opened the door for a relatively large publishing effort for Catholic materials on the European presses (Collinson, Hunt, and Walsham, 2002, 46).

When wealthy patrons and concerned clergy in Wales began to push for Welsh books, the European print industry was an attractive option. European printing was more advanced and higher in quality than English printing, for the most part, and the greater number of European presses drove the prices for printing lower. But there were complications, as well. Due to the difficulty of the Welsh language, Welsh speakers had to travel to Europe to oversee the printing process. This travel, along with the cost to import the printed books, cut deeply into any cost savings made by printing in Europe.

More problematic, however, was the danger involved with the types of materials that were desired in Welsh. Just like the printers themselves, the materials were often politically dissident or Catholic and, therefore, contraband once they were imported to Wales. Possessing and distributing Catholic publications was seen as a treasonous act and could be punished by death. The Stationers' charter gave them the power to seize and destroy illegally printed materials, but it also provided power to do the same to dangerous or seditious texts. In a politically and religiously tense time, imported books from Europe were scrutinized carefully, taxed heavily, and too often seized or destroyed (Williams, 1998: 48).

Even with the complications involved with printing, Welsh books were printed in Europe. Of the roughly sixty Welsh books that were printed before 1604, perhaps seven to ten of them were printed in Milan or Paris (Gruffydd, 1998: 62).

4.4 Printing in Caves

> *Inside the hill without much fear,*
> *With the wooden press the men are printing*
> *The pleasant book, with much praise*
> *Throughout Christendom,*
> *The Drych Cristianogawl.*
> —*Mawl Penrhyn*, by William Pugh[21]

Welsh resistance to the new political, linguistic, and religious orders in the country were not restricted to official efforts. Like many recusants throughout the United Kingdom, Welsh Catholics maintained their religion as much as possible, even when they had to do so in secret. Clandestine Catholic services were carried out in hidden locations, and secret rooms and tunnels were built in Catholic houses to help priests hide or escape arrest or persecution. On the whole, Welsh Catholics were not targeted as much as their English

---

[21] Kelly, 2014: 10.

counterparts, but they were prohibited from having houses of worship and from producing any publications that were not in line with the Anglican Church, especially those that were published in Welsh.

One solution was to turn to European printers, who would print Catholic materials in Welsh that could be smuggled into the country and distributed to Welsh Catholics. A more daring solution was to set up secret presses and produce Welsh Catholic materials in the country. The problem with this was that printing presses were large, heavy, and difficult to hide, and they required bulky bundles of paper, type, and ink to operate. Nevertheless, in the late 1500s, a handful of secret presses (perhaps as many as five) were set up in Wales, often funded and protected by Catholic gentry (Gruffydd, 1998: 62).

One of the most important of these secret presses was established by Robert Gwyn and Robert Pugh. Initially, the press was in Pugh's home at Penrhyn Creuddyn. After a raid in 1586, however, Pugh, Gwyn, and several other Catholic recusants fled to Rhiwledyn, just outside of Llandudno in the north of Wales. There they set up their press in a cave, where they lived with six other men and worked on printing in secret for more than seven months.

The major work published in the cave was *Y Drych Cristionogawl* (*The Christian Mirror*). This book is one of the earliest Welsh-language printed works and is the earliest surviving book printed in Wales. To avoid discovery of their secret cave, Gwyn and Pugh falsified the title page, attributing the authorship to Rhosier Smith, who was in continental Europe; providing a date of 1585 (rather than 1587); and naming Rouen as the place of publication (Kelly, 2014: 13). All of this was to protect their printing press and obscure their own involvement.

In the spring of 1587, locals from nearby communities saw smoke coming from the cave and went to investigate. The eight men living in the cave were arrested, and the printed pages and lead type were thrown into the ocean (the press itself was too heavy to move). Most of the men were released or escaped; some went to Europe where they could live as Catholics. One, the priest William Davies, was drawn and quartered in 1593 after steadfastly refusing to recant his Catholic faith (Kelly, 2014: 18).

The secret presses were a major rebellion against the active censorship of the Protestant crown. By printing Catholic materials in Welsh in Wales, Gwyn and Pugh were actually committing three separate crimes: Catholic materials were expressly forbidden; the Welsh language needed special approval to be used; and printing outside of London and away from the control of the Stationers was illegal. And yet the Catholics printing in caves was only one of the Welsh rebellions in the many years of official suppression.

Although we have records of things being printed, including prayer books, pamphlets, and apologetics for Catholicism, few of these materials survived. Many were destroyed by zealous Protestant officials when the secret presses were discovered. Others were hidden, but have been lost to time and later conflicts. But the stories of the Catholic secret presses are an important chapter in the history of Welsh rebellion through publishing.

5 The Industrial Era

Old King Coal was a merry old soul:
'I'll move the world,' quoth he;
'My England's high, and rich, and great,
But greater she shall be!'
And he call'd for the pick, and he call'd for the spade,
And he call'd for his miners bold;
'And it's dig,' he said, 'in the deep, deep earth;
You'll find my treasures better worth
Than mines of Indian gold!'

—Charles Mackay[22]

Industrialization came early to Wales. There were major copper and iron works as early as the 1580s, and the country was a major producer of coal for all of Great Britain by the mid-1700s. As demand for coal and metals increased with the increasing industrialization of the British Empire, more and more workers were employed in Wales, including both the native Welsh and immigrants from Ireland, Scotland, England, and other countries. Hundreds of thousands of people worked in the mines and associated support businesses in Wales, while most of the profits flowed out of Wales to London-based management.

In the fifty or so years before the recognized beginning of the Industrial Revolution, Wales went through an important, but delayed, revolution of its own: the advent of printing. In the late seventeenth century, Parliament finally relaxed the stranglehold of the Stationers on printing, and the first legal press was established in Wales in 1718. This marked the beginning of a new era of publishing in Wales, but it also coincided with social, political, and religious upheavals brought on by the powers of the press and the forces of industrialization that transformed the country.

[22] Mackay, 1876: 565.

5.1 Printing in Wales

If you could set up an honest Printing office, you would soon have all the business of Wales. —Edward Williams[23]

When the Stationers received their charter in 1557, printing in England was restricted to London and Cambridge. Legal printing locations were expanded to include Oxford in 1586, in part to serve the Welsh market. Beginning in 1660, those restrictions began to be relaxed further, and legal printing presses could be established outside of the three main centers. This didn't mean there was total freedom for printers. Parliament maintained tight control on what was published through the Licensing Act of 1662, which was designed to regulate the spread of printing presses and to prevent the publication of treasonous or seditious materials.

Even with the lifted restrictions on the locations of presses, it wasn't until 1718 that Isaac Carter established the first official press in the little village of Adpar in Western Wales, about seventeen miles north of Carmarthen. It's unclear why Carter established his press in Adpar, a fairly small rural community away from the main population centers (Hopkins, n.d.). The first legal publication from a press in Wales was a ballad by Alban Thomas about the difficulty of quitting smoking entitled "Cân o Senn i'w hen Feistr Tobacco" ("A Song from Senn to His Old Master Tobacco"). This short publication was followed by longer books, including "*Dwysfawr Rym Buchedd Grefyddol* ('The Great Power of the Christian Life') in 1722 and *Y Cristion Cyffredin* ('The Ordinary Christian') in 1724" (Hopkins, n.d.). Other than those few books, Carter's press, like most of the early presses in Wales, published primarily short works on religion and morality in the Welsh language. By 1725, Carter moved his press into Carmarthen, where the larger population and the more established industries could support his printing endeavors. Carmarthen became somewhat of a center for the Welsh book printing industry, thanks to Carter's press and to the printer Nicholas Thomas. Thomas was especially influential in creating business models for the Welsh printing market, including subscription publishing and trade distribution of books (Rees, 1998: 124).

---

[23] Rees, 1998: 126.

After Carter's press opened the door to printing in Wales, small printing shops began to be established in the larger cities and towns. The barriers to printing were still prohibitive, however, and many of the early printing shops failed. Presses, type, and paper were expensive, and the process of printing was difficult and labor-intensive. Most of the early presses in Wales focused on printing professional documents, like invoices and receipts, along with posters, pamphlets, newspapers, poetry, and short fiction and essays, which could be quickly produced and sold for a profit. In general, they left book-length materials to the more established and better funded presses in England.

In spite of the expenses and challenges, there were clear benefits for Welsh printers, especially as the demand for printing grew. In an 1817 letter to his son, Edward Williams wrote, "The fair and legal profits of printing are very great, without embezzling the Authors profits: if you could set up an honest Printing office, you would soon have all the business of Wales: at least of South Wales" (Williams, quoted in Rees, 1998: 126). As the market grew, the opportunities expanded, and many print shops were established throughout Wales, often with close ties to each other and to other shops in England and Ireland. Rees argues that in Wales "members of the book trade were frequently either personally acquainted or linked by blood ties" (Rees, 1998: 127).

At the same time presses were finally being established in Wales, there were major changes happening in the publishing industry in the entirety of Britain. For the first few centuries of printing, the power in the industry had belonged to the printers, who were involved in all stages of publishing, from authorship and translation to physical printing to marketing and selling. In the early eighteenth century, new publishing models, helped in part by a new copyright system, shifted the power away from the printers to newly formed publishing companies. Authorship, book creation, translation, marketing, and bookshops gradually became separated from the physical work of printing. By the mid-eighteenth century, the structure of the modern publishing industry had been established, with powerful publishers and much diminished (but still important) printers.

The old model of printer-centric publishing did not disappear immediately, however. In fact, in emerging markets and smaller communities, like the ones in Wales and in the United States, the time period from roughly 1750 until the turn of the twentieth century was something of a golden age for print shops. Small print shops sprang up throughout the villages, towns, and cities. Many of these shops printed limited runs of short texts or newspapers, but a surprising number of also tackled the larger task of publishing the occasional book. And most of the small-shop printers continued the centuries-old tradition of being authors, editors, and translators as well as printers.

The varied tasks and high expectations of nineteenth-century printers can be found in a number of manuals that were produced in the 1800s and were widely used in print shops throughout Britain and the United States. In *The Printer*, produced in 1833, the author lays out the expectations for a successful compositor:

> A lad who desires to become a compositor must have had at least a good common education, he must have been taught reading, writing, arithmetic, and be able to read different hand-writings with facility, though in this he is greatly improved by his practice in his business. A little instruction in drawing is also of use, at least so far as to enable him to discover and appreciate symmetry of form and accuracy of proportion. (quoted in Rummonds, 2004: 43)

In the 1836 *The Printer's Guide*, these requirements are expanded for a printer:

> It is of great advantage to a printer to have some knowledge of the arts and sciences, the Greek, the Latin, the French, and the Spanish languages. All this may not be in the power of many to acquire to any degree of proficiency; yet, a limited knowledge of them will be found of great service. But what is essential, nay, indispensable, to constitute a good printer, is a thorough knowledge of grammar.
> (quoted in Rummonds, 2004: 118)

And finally, the 1838 *The Printer's Manual* includes detailed qualifications for a print shop proofreader (along with some pointed commentary about authors):

> A reader ought to be well versed in all the peculiarities of the
> English tongue – its idioms, its true genius, and singular
> adaptation to that variety of expression in which we embody
> our thoughts, and pourtray the human intellect. . . . Many, even
> of our first-rate authors, are too apt, in the warmth of discus-
> sion, the flights of speculation, and the laborious exercise of
> thinking powers, to pass over, unobserved, those deviations
> from pure diction and strict grammatical accuracy, which they
> have imperceptibly acquired the habit of falling into, by their
> ordinary conversation with mankind.
>
> (quoted in Rummonds, 2004: 67)

While the printer's manuals may be a bit unrealistic in their expectations
of nineteenth-century workers (and, indeed, the manuals tend to use
quite a lot of space moralizing about the dangers of drink and the virtues
of hard work), they do show that printers were considered educated and
thoughtful participants in the creation of good publications, rather than
simply technical laborers. These expectations were common in Wales,
where an 1820 advertisement for pressmen demanded "a steady, sober
man, who understands both the English and Welsh languages, and can
work at Case and Press," and an 1811 advertisement for apprentices
required "Young men who have had a classical education, and understand the Welsh language" (quoted in Rees, 1998: 131).

In Wales, where legalized printing was new, most of the print
shops operated under the old model. Of course authors were sending
books to the publishers in England, but there was still a significant
amount of printing happening in Wales that was unique to the
political, religious, and cultural situation in the country. While most
of the print shops were focused on printing shorter materials, some of
those early Welsh printers continued the tradition of translating and
printing popular works or writing and printing their own materials in
the Welsh language. Even so, "It is interesting to note that for
printing purposes, Welsh was regarded as a foreign language even
in Wales itself, John Painter charging two shillings per sheet extra"
(Rees, 1998: 132).

The expansion of printing outside of England increased the output of Welsh books. While the total number of Welsh books published before 1700 is perhaps less than 200 (Williams, 1998: 49), roughly 1,200 Welsh books were published in the eighteenth century (Hopkins, n.d.). This pales in comparison to the hundreds of thousands of books being printed in England, but it still represents a significant uptick in Welsh book production, especially when you consider that many of those Welsh books were printed in small, traditional shops.

Over the course of the eighteenth century, printing in Wales continued to expand as restrictions were eased and materials became cheaper. Significantly, the majority of the materials being printed were in Welsh, and covered a wide range of religious, political, and social topics. These publications preserve the history of Wales, but they also capture Welsh society in the early stages of the Industrial Revolution. These Welsh publications are catalogued in *Libri Walliae*, which was published by the National Library of Wales in 1987, with a supplement in 2001 (see Rees, 1987; and Parry, 2001). Research after 2001 has turned up additional printed Welsh documents in European collections, further expanding our understanding of early Welsh printing. Even so, the biggest revolution for Welsh printing would not start until the introduction of the iron handpress in 1800.

5.2 The Invention of the Iron Handpress

The exercise of pulling the press bar is not as healthful an one as might be supposed. —1882 Printer's Manual[24]

Gutenberg's original design for the printing press endured for centuries, with only minor modifications, such as improved use of levers and screws to make the process faster and easier. But until 1800, the basic model for the printing press was the same as the Gutenberg original: A large, heavy wooden frame to hold the mechanisms of printing. These presses were unwieldy and hard to transport, and they were often built, assembled, and maintained inside the print shop by the printer himself. The Gutenberg

---

[24] Quoted in Rummonds, 2004: 52.

press was a workhorse, but its wooden parts required frequent maintenance and replacement.

The press was also slow and difficult to use. Printing involved back-breaking labor and extreme patience. *Practical Printing*, a printer's manual from 1882, described the difficulties of the labor:

> The exercise of pulling the press bar is not as healthful an one as might be supposed. A large number of pressmen are ruptured, and there is much mortality among the class from heart-disease caused by too protracted and too violent exertion of the upper part of the body.
>
> (quoted in Rummonds, 2004: 52)

At top speed, a Gutenberg press could only print about 240 sheets per hour (depending, of course, on the speed of the workers). Considering that a book of 300 pages requires 19 sheets (with a 16-page signature), the process of producing even a small run of a published book was slow and laborious. Large print shops had several presses operating at the same time, which required a large number of press operators, typesetters, proofreaders, and apprentices.

In the late 1700s, Charles Stanhope, 3rd Earl Stanhope, a member of Parliament and scientist, began experimenting with revisions to the Gutenberg press. His goal was to use modern techniques to make the press more efficient and easier to produce. The result was the first iron handpress, introduced in 1800. The new press was smaller and made use of springs and levers to double the speed of printing and increase the size of the printing area. The iron handpress was more reliable and more accessible, and even though it was three to four times as expensive as its wooden predecessor, it required little assembly and could withstand heavier use (Rummonds, 2004: 102).

The result was something of a heyday for small printing houses. Printers took advantage of the new iron presses, along with manufactured typefaces, ink, and paper (all three of which earlier printers produced in-shop) to create a huge number of documents, most in small print runs. Printing, which for the most part had been confined to urban areas, became more attainable for rural villages, and small shops were set up throughout the United Kingdom to produce local newsletters, pamphlets, almanacs, and religious materials. Some presses would also produce short runs of books, using a subscription model (first adopted in Wales by the printer Nicholas Thomas in 1723 [Rees, 1998: 124]), where customers would receive one signature of the book at a time and could bring the entire book back to the printer or to an associated bookbinder to be bound when all of the signatures were published.

As new printing technologies were introduced, including rotary presses and steam-powered presses, the small print shops benefited even more. The price of iron handpresses dropped, and there were used presses and second-hand typefaces available on the market. In Wales, which in general lagged about twenty years behind in publishing technologies, the real printing boom started in about 1820 as the small iron handpresses filtered into the towns and villages.

The introduction of the iron handpress coincided with several significant societal changes. First, the shift in power away from the large printers to the publishing companies that took place in the eighteenth and nineteenth centuries opened up a space for small print shops to produce original materials in small runs and not be in competition with the larger printers, which were now focused on producing large runs of books.

Second, the restrictive rules surrounding printing began to be eased. Laws that restricted printing to the Stationers' Company were relaxed in the 1600s, and heavy restrictions on paper, ink, and other printing supplies were lifted. These changed laws made small print shops both legal and economically viable. Additionally, laws surrounding what could be printed and in what languages were changed or relaxed, resulting in a more open environment for printing political, social, and religious commentary.

Third, the supplies for printing were industrialized. Paper, the single most expensive part of printing, was being produced in greater amounts, thanks to the mechanized paper-making process invented by the Fourdrinier brothers in the early 1800s (the patent was granted in 1806, but the brothers had been working on the machine for some time by then) (Underwood, 1807: 327). There were several paper mills in Wales during the nineteenth century, but it is unclear whether they produced print-quality paper (according to Rees, Welsh paper was "possibly too superior and too expensive for general use" [1988: 127]). The reduced cost of the production of paper was offset by onerous duties, which were increased by the government several times after the 1780s. Nevertheless, it was cheaper and easier to get paper in the 1800s than it had ever been before.

In addition to the ease of obtaining paper, printers could order metal type and ink, which was being produced on an industrial scale by suppliers throughout Europe and Britain. Welsh printers still had to struggle with the unique challenges of printing the Welsh language, which has twenty-eight characters and eight digraphs. Many printers, as they had done from the beginning of print, made do with the readily available Latin type. They were aided by the secondhand market for quality type. These changes to the availability of printing supplies reduced the barriers to entry in creating a printing shop and shrunk the day-to-day operating costs of the shops.

Finally, the forces of the Industrial Revolution created conflicts between the working classes and the wealthy merchants and nobility. Violent revolts rocked the working-class areas of Great Britain and its colonies, fueled in part by incendiary ideas shared in posters, flyers, pamphlets, and books produced by small print shops. One eighteenth-century historian wrote of the American Revolution: "In establishing American independence, the pen and press had merit equal to that of the sword" (Ramsay, 1990: 633–4). In a society that was becoming more literate, more access to printed materials meant more ideas were shared that created more opportunities for rebellion against oppressive forces.

For Wales, all of these societal changes began to come to a head in the 1820s. Small print shops sprang up in the industrial cities and smaller towns, and they printed radical new ideas. Print shops run by worker's organizations gave voice to the discontent of the coal miners, who worked life-threatening jobs and lived in crushing poverty. They printed news about mine accidents, notices of strikes, and reports of unfair treatment and injustice. The presses also shared new ideas about philosophy and religion, and pushed a revived concept of Welsh nationalism. The violence in Wales in the early- to mid-nineteenth century was a result of a whole number of oppressive conditions, but it was fomented and spread by the availability of small iron handpresses.

5.3 Political and Social Printing

Books are not written, produced, or read in a vacuum; they reflect underlying changes in society which, in turn, shape and govern the needs and aspirations of the people. —Geraint H. Jenkins[25]

The eighteenth century was a time of unprecedented change for European countries. Devastating wars between Britain and France followed by the American and French revolutions changed how people viewed governments and the power of traditional monarchies. This, combined with the early decades of the Industrial Revolution, a rise in literacy, changes to education, and the spread of new religions, led to a period of social unrest and demands for lasting reforms.

After more than two centuries of book production, there were only a few hundred Welsh books. But in the second half of the eighteenth century, Welsh publishing exploded and expanded into new topics. Where Welsh books had traditionally been very conservative and focused on religion, they increasingly began to turn to more radical ideas. This was especially the case in the fallout of the French Revolution. In the 1790s alone, more than 600 Welsh books were published, many of which "deplored the damaging effects of power and privilege, tithes and rack-rents, evangelical religion, and creeping Anglicization" (Jenkins, 1998: 119). As more presses became available in Wales, more of these radical ideas were published and placed in the hands of the people.

By the end of the eighteenth century, "virtually every town of any consequence in Wales possessed at least one printing press" (Jenkins, 1998: 119). With the invention and spread of the iron handpress, the number of presses grew exponentially, and with them, the number of publications. Hundreds of general interest and specialty periodicals were published; local newspapers were established; books were printed, copied, translated, and adapted; and pamphlets, posters, and political and religious propaganda were produced.

---

[25] Jenkins, 1998: 119.

The publishing output of the Welsh presses was prodigious, and much of it was focused on the working class. As one writer observed in 1865, toward the beginning of the Welsh Renaissance, "When we look at Welsh literature, we can regard it as the literature of the working classes. It is entirely in the hands of the workers and Ministers of the Gospel, and most of those ministers have at one time been workers with literary interests" (quoted in Walters, 1998: 207). The working-class presses of Wales in the nineteenth century were at odds with the traditional presses that had been controlled by upper class elites. The religion of the press was nonconformist; the politics of the press were revolutionary; and the literature of the press was distinctively Welsh and working class.

The National Library of Wales has an online database of hundreds of periodicals from the nineteenth century, representing over a million pages of text (Welsh Journals, n.d.). There were religious journals, Welsh nationalist journals, and a large number of literary journals connected to the Welsh Renaissance of the late nineteenth century. In the early entries in the database, however, there are many political and social journals that explore (or condemn) working-class issues.

There were also books and pamphlets that addressed both sides of the violent uprisings of the 1830s. The Merthyr Rising, the Newport Rising, and the Rebecca Riots inspired books with titles such as *Exposition of the Principles & Objects of the Carmarthen Working Men's Association*, published by Hugh Williams in 1838 in response to a piece in *Seren Gomer*; *Riots in South Wales: An Address to the Working Classes of Wales, on the Late Occurrences at Newport*, published by One of the People in 1839; and *Ymddiddan rhwng Mr. Bowen, deiliad ffyddlon i'r Frenhines a William Thomas, siartist* ("Conversation between Mr. Bowen, Loyal Follower of the Queen and William Thomas, Chartist"), published by Mr. Bowen in 1839.

Yet for every book or pamphlet published in support of the labor movement, there were books and pamphlets published in English and Welsh to convince the working class "that the existing order of things was in essence acceptable; by working hard and living frugally, they could hope to rise in the world" (Davies, 2007b: 428). The most influential of these was the 1859 *Self Help*, by Samuel Smiles, which encouraged the development of an aristocracy of labor, based on learned skill and diligent effort. Instead of fomenting revolt, these kinds of publications inspired the founding of craft unions, which used long apprenticeships and an opposition to strikes to build successful relationships between management and workers.

The publications that came off of the press in the mid-nineteenth century were part of the larger conversation in Wales about social unrest, loyalty to the Crown, Welsh nationalism, and the role of the Welsh language in a nation (and soon a world) dominated by English. These conversations would continue through the nineteenth and twentieth centuries, though they would be further shaped by the role of of Wales's distinctive religious traditions and the 1847 publication of the Parliamentary Blue Books.

5.4 Religious Printing

> *Oh, the Press! oh, the Press! 'tis the mightiest gift*
> *That Heaven to mortals has ever bestow'd*
> —W. G. Miles[26]

Decades of political and social changes were accompanied by a renewed interest in religion. In the late eighteenth century and the early nineteenth century, the various sects of Christianity began large-scale efforts to entice the populace to re-embrace religion. Missionary efforts by Methodists, Baptists, and Unitarians were met by increased efforts by Lutherans, Anglicans, and Catholics and challenged by the organization and growth of new religions, including the Quakers, The Church of Jesus Christ of Latter-day Saints (the Mormons), the Jehovah's Witnesses, and the Seventh-Day Adventists. While some of the missionary zeal was directed toward the colonies in the expanding European empires, equal or more effort was put into converting Christians to specific sects in the hearts of Christian countries.

The waves of religious revival that rolled through Europe, the United Kingdom, and the United States in the early 1800s were accompanied by mountains of printed materials – tracts, pamphlets, books, scriptural translations, and hymnals – designed to attract potential converts. While early

---

[26] Miles, 1856: 4.

religious printing efforts were interdenominational, by the middle of the nineteenth century religious societies "moved away from such ecumenical endeavors and began to show more faith in, and commitment to, denominational printing enterprises to bring about the conversion of their wayward fellow citizens" (Gutjahr, 2007: 194).

The various Protestant sects created the most dominant religious print cultures, but the Catholics and Jews were also very active in publishing. New religious movements, such as the Mormons, the Jehovah's Witnesses, and the Seventh-Day Adventists, relied on strategically placed small print shops to spread their gospel messages and win converts. Many of the churches "placed a messianic faith in the power of the press" (Gutjahr, 2007: 194). One Welsh Mormon convert wrote in 1856:

> Oh, the Press! oh, the Press! 'tis the mightiest gift
> That Heaven to mortals has ever bestow'd;
> 'Tis the handmaid of truth, with whose pow'r it will lift
> Our darken'd and poor human nature to God.
> An epoch was formed when its hist'ry began –
> Tho' Satan, 'twas said, to its being gave birth –
> It does more to enlighten and civilize man
> Than all the philosophy known upon earth.
>
> (Miles, 1856: 4)

In the view of many nineteenth-century printers, the press was not simply a means of producing printed messages. It was a divine gift, provided to "turn the unfaithful multitudes toward Christ" (Gutjahr, 2007: 195). This religious fervor dominated the printed discourse in many local shops throughout the nineteenth century. This religious movement was especially powerful in Wales after about 1820. Socioeconomic conditions had moved many people to seek out religion, and a revived sense of Welsh national pride led many outside of Anglicanism. In fact, "more than 80 per cent of the country was recorded in the 1851 religious census as being outside the established church" (Black and Macraild, 2003: 193). The adoption of the iron handpress coincided with religious changes, and many local print shops were owned or funded by religious organizations.

One example of this religious fervor in printing was in Rhydybont, where the Reverend John Jones, a Protestant minister, owned a press and employed John Sylvanus Davis as his printer. Jones used the press to print tracts and newsletters for his congregation. Davis, as was the case with most village printers, had a huge role in the production of the text. An 1838 printer's manual explains part of the role of a printer:

> By his practical acquaintance with the mechanical depart-
> ment of the business, he will be better able to detect those
> manifold errata which, unperceived by the mere man of
> learning and science, lie lurking, as it were, in a thousand
> different forms, in every sheet; and, if overlooked, evince
> a carelessness and inattention to our labours, that must
> always offend the just taste and professional discernment
> of all true lovers of correct and beautiful typography.
>
>   (quoted in Rummonds, 2004: 67)

Learning "the mechanical department" helped printers control the quality and appearance of the printing work. At the same time, however, they were taught to control the quality of the content. Nineteenth-century small-shop printers were also authors and editors; and in many cases, they would also determine the use and placement of punctuation. Therefore, the apprentices were required "to be well versed in all the peculiarities of the English tongue – its idioms, its true genius, and singular adaptation to that variety of human expression in which we embody our thoughts, and portray the human intellect" (Rummonds, 2004: 67). Maintaining the quality of both appearance and content was considered a vital part of printing. For John Davis, this meant that he was a silent editor and sometimes author of Reverend Jones' work.

In 1846, Reverend Jones' brother Dan returned from the United States, where he had converted to The Church of Jesus Christ of Latter-day Saints, more commonly known as Mormonism. Dan Jones had been called by the Mormon prophet Joseph Smith to return to Wales and lead the missionary efforts there. One of Jones' first endeavors was to begin printing *Prophwyd y Jubili* ("The Prophet of the Jubilee"), a Welsh-language monthly periodical, which Reverend Jones allowed him to print on his press, with the assistance of John Davis.

After the first issue, *Prophwyd y Jubili* was published monthly, and it was augmented by the printing of Mormon tracts that explained the new religion and responded to criticisms. Mormonism was one of the fastest-growing religions in Wales, and by 1848 the new religion was seen as a grave threat by the other congregations in the country, particularly the more traditional Anglican congregations. Although Reverend Jones continued to allow Dan to use his press, he began printing vicious attacks on Mormonism in his own tracts and newsletters.

The same press, working day and night, printed attacks on Mormons and defenses of Mormons, with one major thing in common: the printer himself. John Davis worked on all of the publications that came off of the Jones press, correcting text and setting type as well as printing the final materials. As Davis began to associate more with the Mormons, he took on a larger role writing responses to criticisms he had typeset and printed earlier in the same day. There is some evidence that Davis also occasionally entered corrections or softened the criticisms of Mormonism in the Reverend Jones' work. Within months, the press had acquired the nickname "the Prostitute Press" for its tireless work in service of two very different religious masters (Dennis, 2002: 46).

This situation played out in villages and cities across Wales. The demand to print religious materials far outstripped the number of printing presses, and religious organizations competed for those resources. As more presses became available in the 1840s and 1850s, churches and missionary organizations bought their own presses to devote to printing religious materials full-time – and for responding to vicious attacks from other faiths with apologetics and attack pieces of their own. As these theological debates intensified, some writers complained of the tone of the publications:

> It is not fitting that such a belligerent attitude should man-
> ifest itself in the writings of religious people. They reproach
> and taunt one another in such controversies, and to a large
> extent lower the standards of the publications. It is a pity that
> people who profess religion should trample on one another
> in such a way. (quoted in Walters, 1998: 201)

John Davis left the Prostitute Press and established his own print shop in Merthyr Tydfil in 1848, where he became the official printer for the Mormon movement in Wales, eventually printing thousands of pages of periodicals, hymnals, and the central Mormon scriptures in both English and Welsh. When he emigrated to the United States, along with many of the Welsh Mormons, he took his printing skills and became part of a core group of Welsh and English printers who established book presses, periodicals, and newspapers throughout the Western United States.

Religious printing, which had been at the heart of Welsh publishing for centuries, dominated the print trade in the nineteenth century. The Independent minister Reverend Cadwaladr Jones edited and printed *Y Dysgedydd* ("The Instructor") beginning in 1821. Congregationalists published *Dysgedydd y Plant* ("The Child's Instructor") beginning in 1871. Anglicans published *Gwyliedydd* ("Watchman"), a Welsh-language weekly with local news and religious information, beginning in 1877. These periodicals were distributed throughout Wales and in the larger cities of England. Smaller religious periodicals and local church newsletters number in the hundreds.

In addition to periodicals and tracts, Welsh printers translated and printed religious books, including new printed editions of the Welsh Bible; new Welsh translations of Job, Psalms, and Proverbs by Anglican Vicar Thomas Briscoe in 1853; Welsh translations of the New Testament by Briscoe in 1894 and the Baptist College William Edwards in 1894; and numerous Psalters. Some of greatest religious contributions came through the Welsh tradition of poetry and song: William Williams of Pantycelyn wrote and printed over 1,000 hymns for the Methodist movement in the late 1700s, including his well-known "Arglwydd, arwain trwy'r anialwch" ("Guide Us, O Thou Great Jehovah"); and John S. Davis wrote and printed hundreds of hymns for the Mormon movement, in both English and Welsh. Welsh-written hymns made their way into hymnals throughout the world and continue to be used in many services today.

6 Resistance and Renaissance

Gwell fy mwthyn fy hun na phlas arall

("Better my own cottage than the palace of another")
—Welsh Proverb[27]

Asserting Welsh identity through language, poetry, laws, or traditions had been an act of resistance since the time Edward I completed the conquest of Wales in the thirteenth century. The seriousness of the resistance depended on the attitudes and responses of the English monarchs and English society. Under Edward I, Welshness was seen as rebellion, and ancient traditions like the eisteddfod were ended or outlawed. Under the Tudor dynasty, some elements of Welsh identity were suppressed, including the Welsh language, *Cyfraith Hywel*, and the independence of Welsh regions and the Marcher lords. On the other hand, Queen Elizabeth I reinstated a national eisteddfod, and she and the other Tudor monarchs incorporated elements of Welsh identity into a new unified kingdom.

The rise of publishing allowed a new form of resistance through Welsh-language books and the publication of Welsh histories, stories, poems, and literature. During the first century of printing in Wales, much of this resistance was passive assertion of Welsh identity. Toward the end of the eighteenth century and the beginning of the nineteenth century, Welsh resistance to English rule become more overt. As discussed in the previous chapter, much of that resistance was directed toward labor disputes and religion. In the mid-nineteenth century, Welsh resistance coalesced around opposition to the Parliamentary Blue Books, which were seen as a great insult – and a frontal assault – on Welsh identity.

Part of the resistance movement in the nineteenth century was built around a revived push for Welsh independence. A larger part and – for publishing at least – a more important part was a renewed sense of Welsh

---

[27] Hemmings, 2019.

language, literature, poetry, and song. This modern Welsh Renaissance produced some of Wales' greatest authors and some of the country's most important contributions to world culture.

Resistance and renaissance were intertwined in Wales – Welsh politics were part of Welsh literature, and Welsh literature drove political movements. In examining the history of modern Welsh publishing, it is impossible to separate the texts from the cultural forces of nineteenth- and twentieth-century Wales. And while the origins of Welsh resistance and renaissance can be traced through centuries, the modern movement started with the Treachery of the Blue Books in 1847.

6.1 Treachery of the Blue Books

The Welsh language is a vast drawback to Wales, and a manifold barrier to the moral progress and commercial prosperity of the people.
—Reports of the Commissioners of Inquiry into the State of Education in Wales[28]

In 1847, the British Government published the three-volume *Reports of the Commissioners of Inquiry into the State of Education in Wales*, more commonly known as the Parliamentary Blue Books. This extensive report was compiled by three English commissioners who, at the request of Coventry MP William Williams, toured Wales and conducted interviews to determine the state of the education system. The Blue Books were highly critical and were met with immediate backlash in Wales, particularly because the commissioners spoke no Welsh and relied on interviews with Anglican clergy in a time when Wales was a hotspot of religious nonconformity. The reports criticized the language, morals, education, and religions of Wales. In one section, the commissioners wrote:

> The Welsh language is a vast drawback to Wales, and a manifold barrier to the moral progress and commercial prosperity of the people. It is not easy to over-estimate its evil effects

---

[28] Reports, vol. 2, 1847: 66.

> ... It dissevers the people from intercourse which would
> greatly advance their civilisation, and bars the access of improv-
> ing knowledge to their minds. (Reports, vol. 2, 1847: 66)

The Welsh people, of course, were infuriated. The bard Robert Jones Derfel responded to the reports with a book-length play titled *Brad y Llyfrau Gleision* ("Treachery of the Blue Books") that was published in 1854. The play presents Wales as "an extremely godly country" (*Brad y Llyfrau Gleision*, n.d.). In the second act, Beelzebub sends three demonic spies to compile a report, and they are aided by treacherous clergy, who enjoy their demonic associations. The title, *Treachery of the Blue Books*, is an allusion to the Treachery of the Long Knives, the legendary sixth-century Anglo-Saxon massacre of Celtic chieftains at a peace conference.

Derfel's play, with its thinly veiled attacks on the English commissioners and the Anglican clergy, captured Welsh anger at the government for the Blue Books. In a country that had been rocked by recent labor riots and economic struggles, the Blue Books seemed like a particularly vicious attack: Wales wasn't poor because its mineral wealth was flowing to the wealthy in London; it was poor because its people were of low character, low intelligence, and low religious morals. Derfel's play helped focus Welsh anger on Parliament, the commissioners, and Anglican clergy.

The publication of the Parliamentary Blue Books and the Welsh response to the reports had long-lasting consequences for Wales. On the one hand, the negative reports in the Blue Books were used to justify further restrictions on the Welsh language and additional English control of Welsh schools. Even among the Welsh people the Blue Books were seen as a humiliation, and some embraced the restrictions on using Welsh in schools and publications and focused instead on learning English language, history, and culture. As historian Geraint H. Jenkins writes, "While the Irish were victims of their history, the Welsh were starved of their own past" (Jenkins, 2007: 216).

On the other hand, the Blue Books united and focused Welsh nationalist movements. Derfel's play, published seven years after the Blue Books, was only one of many nationalist responses, many of which took the form of political pamphlets and newsletters that pushed back against the English assessment of Wales. In addition, the Blue Books also drove a renewed interest in the poetry, songs, literature, and traditions of Wales. The Welsh nationalist movement grew along with a Welsh Renaissance that created some of the most important Welsh contributions to the modern world, both in English and in Welsh.

6.2 Welsh Nationalist Printing

A nation is swiftly overcome if its spirit is weak; but with unyielding determination it can vanquish powers that appear to be utterly invincible.
—Gwynfor Evans[29]

Welsh nationalism predated the publication of the Blue Books, of course. In fact, there were surges of Welsh nationalism and pushes for independence going back to the earliest days of Anglo-Welsh relations. But the rise of printing and the publication of the Blue Books gave a new voice to Welsh nationalism in the nineteenth century, with more radical political philosophies than had been seen before.

The earliest nationalist publications were associated with religion. The people of Wales, who had always been resistant to Anglicanism from the time of Henry VIII, saw the Anglican Church as a foreign institution and a tool for the subjugation of Welsh culture and the Welsh language. Even with the official publication of the Bible and other religious materials, beginning in the sixteenth century, the Welsh continued to view religion and nationalism together as twin pillars of resistance to English oppression.

Consequently, three of the earliest and most radical Welsh nationalism periodicals were published by Congregationalist ministers: *Y Diwygiwr* ("The Reformer"), published by David Rees from 1835–1865; *Yr Amserau* ("The Times"), published by William Rees from 1846–1859 and then merged into a new publication called *Baner ac Amserau Cymru*, which lasted until 1971; and *Cronicl y cymdeithasau crefyddol* ("The Chronicle of Religious Societies"), published by Samuel Roberts from 1843–1910.

---

[29] Evans, 1974.

Of the three Congregationalist publishers, William Rees is the one who perhaps best exemplifies the nineteenth-century Welsh nationalist movement. Rees was appointed a minister in 1831, and preached throughout Wales and into Liverpool during the 1830s and 1840s. But Rees was also an author and a poet. He won a prize at the Brecon eisteddfod "for a *cywydd* on the victory at Trafalgar and the death of Nelson" in 1826 (Davies, 1959), and he published a huge number of poems, stories, and books during his life, under his bardic name Gwilym Hiraethog. Rees's most influential political publication, however, was *Yr Amserau*, which dealt with religious issues, but also covered "politics, the Corn Laws, education, the Oxford movement and the Papacy" (*Yr Amserau*, n.d.).

Like many of his contemporaries in the nationalist movement, Rees called for a revival of Welsh culture and language and a move toward political independence. But he did not see Welsh nationalism as an isolated movement in the world. Rather, Rees placed the efforts in Wales as part of a global radicalist movement. In *Yr Amserau*, Rees wrote about European conflicts, including the Italian war of independence and the Hungarian war with Austria. He also authored a book entitled *Aelwyd F'ewythr Robert*, which argued for the abolition of slavery in the United States (Davies, 1959). The worldwide efforts were connected to the Welsh efforts through their struggles against the same forces: the oppressions of traditional religions, the injustices of colonialism, and the troubling power of governments and monarchies.

Although the radical periodicals had wide circulation in Wales, their effects on public opinion were mixed. As the political and social situations in Wales settled into a relative calm in the late nineteenth century, there was less of an immediate impetus to drive for Welsh independence. In addition, the Blue Books and the English school system had a debilitating effect on attitudes toward the Welsh language and Welsh independence. The Welsh language had been cast as backward since Henry VIII, and the Blue Books reinforced that with the conclusion that Welsh was "a vast drawback to Wales, and a manifold barrier to the moral progress and commercial prosperity of the people" (Reports, vol. 2, 1847: 66). In the mid-nineteenth century, the Welsh language was already declining in use; by the census of 1911, it had fallen into minority language status for the first time in the country's history. The eastern parts of Wales were almost entirely English, and the Welsh-speaking areas were shrinking each year.

In the 1920s, concern for the preservation of Welsh language and culture led to a revival of Welsh nationalism. Several different Welsh movements came together symbolically at the 1925 National Eisteddfod to form Plaid Cymru, with the "principal aim . . . of a Welsh-speaking Wales" (Davies, 2007b: 532), along with more radical goals to cut ties with Parliament and other British political parties. One of the first efforts was to begin a new publishing effort with *Y Ddraig Goch* ("The Red Dragon"), a monthly periodical that provided essays and party news in Welsh. Soon, however, the nationalist efforts shifted to fighting for a Welsh-language presence on the newer media of radio and television.

On the whole, radical Welsh nationalism played a fairly small role in the history of Welsh publishing. Of much more importance was a different sort of resistance: The revival of Welsh poetry and literature through numerous periodicals and books published in the second half of the nineteenth century.

6.3 The Welsh Renaissance

By restoring Wales to her rightful place we will strengthen the Welshman's character, purify his soul, nourish his genius, and enrich his life.
—Owen M. Edwards[30]

In the middle of the nineteenth century, the social, economic, religious, and political changes that had changed the nature of Wales over the previous hundred years began to settle into a new reality. The social unrest and violent uprisings had largely ended by the mid-1840s, and while workers still struggled, they forming unions and engaging politically rather than taking to the streets to fight. The demand for coal remained high. The religious fervor of the early nineteenth century had evolved past some of the petty theological squabbles. All of these changes came together to create a revived interest in Welsh history, language, culture, and literature.

---

[30] Walters, 1998: 206.

It could be argued that one watershed moment came at the modern revival of the eisteddfod in 1819, where the oldest surviving bardic chair was awarded to the winner. That date is a little deceiving, however, because eisteddfodau had never really been entirely abandoned. The ancient tradition of the bardic contest had gone through ebbs and flows of popularity (and sponsorship) on the large scale, but had always been a part of informal, community celebrations. The important thing about the 1819 eisteddfod is that it was the public debut of the pseudo-druidic ceremonies advocated by the bard Iolo Morganwg and his organization the Gorsedd. It invigorated public interest in the eisteddfod and is seen as the origin of the National Eisteddfod, which officially began in 1861.

Perhaps just as important to the revival of eisteddfodau in Welsh society, in 1822 all of the poems from the competition began to be published. This was a major development, because the oral nature of the bardic competitions was almost sacred. But the public devoured the opportunity to read the traditional poetry, and winners of the eisteddfodau became local celebrities. The eisteddfodau continued to grow in popularity. Today there are international, national, and local eisteddfodau in Welsh communities throughout the world. The National Eisteddfod draws more than 6,000 contestants and over 150,000 spectators (Eisteddfod, n.d.).

The publication of poetry was just the first step in the Welsh Renaissance. As the availability of printing increased, the number of Welsh-language publications increased, and by the middle of the century an increasing number of those were focused on literature. As has been noted earlier, the majority of the Welsh presses in the nineteenth century were owned and operated by religious organizations. While those presses focused initially on producing pamphlets and religious tracts, they soon turned to more diverse subjects. As Walters argues, "publication of a literary quarterly was regarded as a sign that a denomination had attained intellectual maturity" (Walters, 1998: 204). The Methodists published *Y Traethodydd* ("The Essayist"), while the Congregationalists published *Yr Adolygydd* ("The Reviewer") and then *Y Beirniad* ("The Critic"). Each of these included essays on a broad range of topics rather than focusing specifically on theology.

In addition to the development of literary periodicals, the nineteenth century also brought with it a renewed interest in the folklore, legends, and myths of Wales. There were new editions of *Le Morte D'Arthur* beginning in 1816, and the *Mabinogion* was translated and published in its entirety for the first time in the 1830s. Although *Le Morte D'Arthur* was in English and the *Mabinogion* was in both Welsh and English, they signaled a revival of interest in the traditions and culture of Wales.

The publication of the Blue Books in 1847 brought furious direct responses, but it also greatly increased the number of periodicals. Walters writes:

> As the Welsh people sought to convince themselves that they were as civilized and cultured as any other nation, education and general knowledge came to be regarded as the keys which opened the door to economic and social advancement and as the means of curing every social ill.
>
> (Walters, 1998: 204)

In post-Blue Book Wales, this effort to "convince themselves" meant establishing monthly, quarterly, and even weekly magazines on every conceivable topic. There were periodicals for the serious essayist, for women, for children, for satirists, for poets, for cartoonists, for musicians, and for storytellers. In the second half of the century, there were several magazines devoted entirely to publishing the poems of the eisteddfodau, including *Taliesin*, which was published from 1859–1861, and *Yr Eisteddfod*, published from 1864–1866.

Most of these periodicals were short-lived (that is not unusual for periodicals, especially those that are dissenting or oppositional; while a few survive and enjoy long-term success, many more last only a few issues). But the periodicals both reflected and built a literary culture that has become a distinguishing feature of modern Wales. This was, in fact, an explicit goal of Owen M. Edwards, one of the most influential nineteenth-century Welsh publishers. In the opening issue of his periodical *Cymru* in 1891, he wrote:

> I believe that nothing will invigorate the Welshman's character as much as the knowledge of his own country's

history. .... What my colleagues and I intend to accomplish with *Cymru* is to trace the history of Wales, relate her traditions, give voice once again to her poets and men of letters, give her heroes their rightful place. And we will accomplish these things because the present age is the age of Wales's education ... by restoring Wales to her rightful place we will strengthen the Welshman's character, purify his soul, nourish his genius, and enrich his life.

(Owen M. Edwards, quoted in Walters, 1998: 206).

The long list of great Welsh authors of the twentieth century owe at least part of their success to the literary and poetic culture that was developed over hundreds of years and finally put into print in the later part of the nineteenth century. During the twentieth century, the presses of Wales decreased in importance, especially as the country entered a long depression after World War I and the decline of the coal industry. But Welsh authors and Welsh books had established an audience that has continued to be served by the publishing houses of England and Scotland.

7 Conclusion: Into the Electronic Age

Cenedl heb iaith, cenedl heb galon.

(A nation without language is a nation without heart.)
—Welsh Proverb[31]

As the twentieth century drew to a close and the twenty-first century began, Wales won several important victories: Welsh was recognized as an official language in 1993, ending centuries of linguistic oppression. The Welsh Assembly was formed in 1999 and the Senedd Cymru in 2006, providing some level of autonomy for the Welsh people. And, in 2011, Welsh was made the official language of Wales, meaning that the official business of the Senedd and the courts of Wales would be conducted in the native language.

For Welsh publishing, the twenty-first century opened new opportunities for Welsh culture, language, and literature. As it did throughout the world, the Internet allowed for expanded publishing efforts in Wales, breaking through the barriers of traditional publishing. Print-on-demand technologies provide more options for independent publishers and self-publishers without the resources to produce and store large print runs of books.

Perhaps most importantly for Welsh publishing, however, the Internet opened the doors to preserving and distributing the great works from hundreds of years of Welsh authors. The National Library of Wales was founded in 1907 with a Royal Charter to collect, preserve, and maintain all materials "which have been or shall be composed in Welsh or any other Celtic language" (source quoted in Madden, 1998: 399). From the early 1980s, the mission of the National Library has included digitizing and distributing their vast collection of Welsh texts. Today, the National Library website provides easy access to *Cyfraith Hywel* and the ancient manuscripts of the *Mabinogion*. Readers anywhere in the world can access a digitized version of *Yny lhyvyr hwnn*, the first printed book in Welsh

---

[31] Hemmings, 2019.

(which has only one surviving copy). There are digital databases of important Welsh publications, Welsh newspapers, and Welsh periodicals, and there are brief biographies of the people who contributed to the history of publishing in Wales. As Madden argues, "the Library's wholehearted participation in the foundation of the Aberystwyth Centre for the Book indicates its strong belief in the past and future significance of the book as a medium for human communication" (Madden, 1998: 404).

In addition to preserving the history of Welsh publishing in the National Library, the Welsh government has committed to promoting new Welsh publishing with the formation of the Welsh Books Council, the Arts Council of Wales, and other foundations and committees, which sponsor and promote the publication of hundreds of Welsh-language books and English books of Welsh interest every year. And, after centuries of working primarily with Latin-based typefaces, in 2015 the Welsh government commissioned a new digital typeface specifically for the Welsh language, which includes all twenty-eight letters and eight digraphs (Wales, 2015). The ancient words, stories, poems, laws, and histories of Wales can now be typed in their original characters.

As we continue into the electronic age, it is worthwhile to look back at the centuries of development that brought us here. For Wales, that means a long history of contributions to society that were sung by the bards, handwritten by medieval monks, printed by the powerful printers of England and Europe, and finally published in Wales by Welsh printers. This history of publishing in Wales is intertwined with the history of Wales, and it is a history of a rich culture and a proud people whose legacies live on in the texts they produced.

References

Arber, E. (1875). *A Transcript of the Registers of the Company of Stationers of London, 1557–1640, Vol. 1.* London: Stationers' Company.

Aronstein, S. (2019). "Beyond the Fields We Know": Wales and Fantasy Literature. In G. Evans and H. Fulton, eds., *The Cambridge History of Welsh Literature.* Cambridge: Cambridge University Press, pp. 619–36.

Barnard, J. and McKenzie, D. F., eds. (2002). *The Cambridge History of the Book in Britain, Vol. 4: 1557–1695.* Cambridge: Cambridge University Press.

Bernard, G. W. (2011). The Dissolution of the Monasteries. *History*, 96 (324), 390–409.

Black, J. and Macraild, D. M. (2003). *Nineteenth-Century Britain.* Houndmills: Palgrave Macmillan.

Bollard, J. K. (2006). *Legend and Landscape of Wales: The Mabinogi.* Llandysul: Gomer.

Bolt, R. (2013). *A Man for All Seasons.* London: Bloomsbury.

Botkin, B. A. (1996). Definitions of Folklore. *Journal of Folklore Research*, 33 (3), 255–64.

Brad y Llyfrau Gleision. (n.d.). *National Library of Wales*, www.library.wales/ digital-exhibitions-space/digital-exhibitions/europeana-rise-of-literacy/ the-blue-books-reports/brad-y-llyfrau-gleision#?c=&m=&s=&cv= 8&xywh=-705%2C-1%2C3287%2C2792, accessed July 9, 2021.

Brehaut, E. (1912). *An Encyclopedist of the Dark Ages: Isidore of Seville.* New York: Columbia University.

Bromwich, R. and Evans, D. S., eds. (2012). *Culhwch ac Olwen.* Cardiff: University of Wales Press.

Cambrensis, G. (2018). *The Description of Wales.* Frankfurt: Outlook Verlag.

Campbell, W. (2012). *Materials for a History of the Reign of Henry VII: From Original Documents Preserved in the Public Record Office*. Cambridge: Cambridge University Press.

Clair, C. (1976). *A History of European Printing*. London: Academic Press.

Collinson, P., Hunt, A., and Walsham, A. (2002). Religious Publishing in England: 1557–1640. In J. Barnard and D. F. McKenzie, eds., *The Cambridge History of the Book in Britain, Vol. 4: 1557–1695*. Cambridge: Cambridge University Press, pp. 29–66.

Cull, M. R. (2014). *Shakespeare's Prince of Wales: English Identity and the Welsh Connection*. Oxford: Oxford University Press.

Davies, J. (2007a). *A History of Wales*, revised ed. London: Penguin.

Davies, S. (2007b). *The Mabinogion*. Oxford: Oxford University Press.

Davies, T. E. (1959). Rees, William (Gwilym Hiraethog; 1802–1883), Independent Minister, Writer, Editor, and Political Leader. *Dictionary of Welsh Biography*, https://biography.wales/article/s-REES-WIL-1802, accessed July 9, 2021.

Delamarre, X. (2003). *Dictionnaire de la Langue Gauloise*, 2nd ed. Arles: Errance, pp. 37–38.

De Lamartine, A. (1854). *Memoirs of Celebrated Characters, Vol. 2*, 2nd ed. London: Richard Bentley.

Dennis, R. D. (2002). Llyfr Mormon: The Translation of the Book of Mormon into Welsh. *Journal of Book of Mormon Studies*, 11, 45–49.

Douglas, D. C. and Rothwell, H. (1996). *English Historical Documents, 1189–1327*. Hove: Psychology Press.

Edwards, E. (2019) Romantic Wales and the Eisteddfod. In G. Evans and H. Fulton, eds., *The Cambridge History of Welsh Literature*. Cambridge: Cambridge University Press, pp. 285–305.

Eisteddfod. (n.d.). The National Eisteddfod of Wales, https://eisteddfod.wales/about-us, accessed July 9, 2021.

Ekwall, E. (1930). Early Names of Britain. *Antiquity*, 4(14), 149–56.

Evans, G. (1974). *Land of My Fathers: 2,000 Years of Welsh History*. Swansea: John Penry Press.

Evans, G. (2019). Tudor London and the Origins of Welsh Writing in English. In G. Evans and H. Fulton, eds., *The Cambridge History of Welsh Literature*. Cambridge: Cambridge University Press, pp. 212–31.

Evans, G. and Fulton, H., eds. (2019). *The Cambridge History of Welsh Literature*. Cambridge: Cambridge University Press.

Feather, J. (2006). *A History of British Publishing*, 2nd ed. London: Routledge.

Ferris, P., ed. (1985). *Dylan Thomas: The Collected Letters*. London: Macmillan.

Fulton, H. (2019). Britons and Saxons: The Earliest Writing in Welsh. In G. Evans and H. Fulton, eds., *The Cambridge History of Welsh Literature*. Cambridge: Cambridge University Press, pp. 26–51.

Gerald of Wales. (1997a). The Description of Wales. *Vision of Britain*, www.visionofbritain.org.uk/travellers/Cambrensis_Desc/31, accessed July 9, 2021.

Gerald of Wales. (1997b). The Itinerary of Archbishop Baldwin through Wales. *Vision of Britain*, www.visionofbritain.org.uk/travellers/Cambrensis_Tour/2, accessed July 9, 2021.

Glyn, I. (2016). Y ty hwn ("This House"). *Literature Wales*, www.literaturewales.org/our-projects/national-poet-wales/cerddi-comisiwn-ifor-ap-glyn/this-house/, accessed July 9, 2021.

Gruffydd, R. G. (1998). The First Printed Books, 1546–1604. In P. H. Jones and E. Rees, eds., *A Nation and Its Books: A History of the Book in Wales*. Aberystwyth: The National Library of Wales and the Aberystwyth Centre for the Book, pp. 55–65.

Guest, C. (1877). *The Mabinogion*. London: Bernard Quaritch.

Gutjahr, P. C. (2007). Diversification in American Religious Publishing. In S. Casper, J. D. Groves, S. W. Nessenbaum and M. Winship, eds.,

A History of the Book in America, Vol. 3: The Industrial Book, 1840–1880. Chapel Hill: University of North Carolina Press, pp. 194–202.

Hemmings, B. (2019). Old Welsh Proverbs, Sayings and Phrases. *Welsh Gift Shop*, https://welshgiftshop.com/blogs/welsh-gift-shop/8681985-old-welsh-proverbs-sayings-and-phrases, accessed July 9, 2021.

Hopkins, M. (n.d.). Wales' First Permanent Printing Press. Why Did It Take So Long? *WordCatcher*, https://wordcatcher.com/wales-first-permanent-printing-press-why-did-it-take-so-long-mel-hopkins, accessed July 9, 2021.

Huws, D. (1998). The Medieval Manuscript. In P. H. Jones and E. Rees, eds., *A Nation and Its Books: A History of the Book in Wales*. Aberystwyth: The National Library of Wales and the Aberystwyth Centre for the Book, pp. 26–39.

Huws, D. (2008). The Welsh Book. In N. Morgan and R. M. Thomson, eds., *The Cambridge History of the Book in Britain, Vol. 2: 1100–1400.* Cambridge: Cambridge University Press, pp. 390–96.

Jenkins, G. H. (1998). The Eighteenth Century. In P. H. Jones and E. Rees, eds., *A Nation and Its Books: A History of the Book in Wales*. Aberystwyth: The National Library of Wales and the Aberystwyth Centre for the Book, pp. 109–22.

Jenkins, G. H. (2007). *A Concise History of Wales*. Cambridge: Cambridge University Press.

Jones, P. H. and Rees, E., eds. (1998). *A Nation and Its Books: A History of the Book in Wales*. Aberystwyth: The National Library of Wales and the Aberystwyth Centre for the Book.

The Juvencus Englynion (1932). *Celtic Literature Collective*, www.maryjones.us/ctexts/juvencus.html, accessed July 9, 2021.

Kelly, J. (2014). *Blessed William Davies, Priest and Publisher*. Manchester: Universe Media Group.

Koch, J. T. (2006). *Celtic Culture*. Santa Barbara: ABC–CLIO.

Laws in Wales Act. (1535). *Legislation.gov.uk*, www.legislation.gov.uk /aep/Hen8/27/26/contents, accessed July 9, 2021.

Laws in Wales Act. (1542). *Legislation.gov.uk*, www.legislation.gov.uk /aep/Hen8/34-35/26/contents, accessed July 9, 2021.

Lee, L. (2015). *I Can't Stay Long*. London: Penguin Classics.

Luft, D. (2019). Commemorating the Past after 1066: Tales from *The Mabinogion*. In G. Evans and H. Fulton, eds., *The Cambridge History of Welsh Literature*. Cambridge: Cambridge University Press, pp. 73–92.

Mackay, C. (1876). *The Poetical Works of Charles Mackay: Now for the First Time Collected Complete in One Volume*. London: Frederick Warne.

Madden, L. (1998). The National Library of Wales and the Future of the Book. In P. H. Jones and E. Rees, eds., *A Nation and Its Books: A History of the Book in Wales*. Aberystwyth: The National Library of Wales and the Aberystwyth Centre for the Book, pp. 399–405.

Malory, T. (1889). *Le Morte D'Arthur*. London: David Nutt. https://quod .lib.umich.edu/c/cme/MaloryWks2/1:23?rgn=div1;view=toc, accessed July 9, 2021.

Miles, W. G. (1856). Second Annual Festival of Deseret Typographical Association. *Deseret News*, February 13, p. 4.

Moore, D. (2005). *The Welsh Wars of Independence*. London: The History Press.

Morgan, W. (1588). Dedication in the Welsh Bible of 1588, translated by A. O. Evans. *National Library of Wales*, www.library.wales/discover/ digital-gallery/printed-material/1588-welsh-bible/english-translation- of-the-dedication-in-the-1588-bible, accessed July 9, 2021.

Morgan, N. and Thomson, R. M., eds. (2008). *The Cambridge History of the Book in Britain, Vol. 2: 1100–1400*. Cambridge: Cambridge University Press.

Nennius. (1848). Historia Brittonum. *The Camelot Project*, https://d.lib .rochester.edu/camelot/text/nennius-history-of-the-britons, accessed July 9, 2021.

Newton, M. (2016). Text: Cyfraith Hywel. *Exploring Celtic Civilizations*, https://exploringcelticciv.web.unc.edu/prsp-record/text-cyfraith-hywel/, accessed July 92021.

Parr, C. (2011). *Katherine Parr: Complete Works and Correspondence*, edited by J. Mueller. Chicago: University of Chicago Press.

Parry, C. (2001). *Libri Walliae: A Catalogue of Welsh Books and Books Printed in Wales 1546-1820: Supplement*. Aberystwyth: National Library of Wales.

Price, A. (2019). Welsh Humanism After 1536. In G. Evans and H. Fulton, eds., *The Cambridge History of Welsh Literature*. Cambridge: Cambridge University Press, pp. 176–93.

Price, J. (1546). *Yny lhyvyr hwnn*. National Library of Wales, www.library.wales/discover/digital-gallery/printed-material/yny-lhyvyr-hwnn/#?c=&m=&s=&cv=&xywh=-400%2C-68%2C2584%2C2195, accessed July 9, 2021.

Pryce, H. (1998). The Origins and the Medieval Period. In P. H. Jones and E. Rees, eds., *A Nation and Its Books: A History of the Book in Wales*. Aberystwyth: The National Library of Wales and the Aberystwyth Centre for the Book, pp. 1–23.

Pughe, W. O. (1795). The Mabinogion, or juvenile amusements, being ancient Welsh romances. *Cambrian Register*, pp. 177–87.

Ramsay, D. (1990). *The History of the American Revolution*, edited by H. Lester Cohen, 2 vols. Indianapolis: Liberty Fund. Originally published in 1789.

Rees, E. (1987). *Libri Walliae: A Catalogue of Welsh Books and Books Printed in Wales 1546-1820*. Aberystwyth: National Library of Wales.

Rees, E. (1998). The Welsh Book Trade from 1718 to 1820. In P. H. Jones and E. Rees, eds., *A Nation and Its Books: A History of the Book in Wales*. Aberystwyth: The National Library of Wales and the Aberystwyth Centre for the Book, pp. 123–33.

Reports of the Commissioners of Inquiry into the State of Education in Wales, 3 Vols. (1847). London: William Clowes and Sons. www.library.wales/digital-exhibitions-space/digital-exhibitions/europeana-rise-of-literacy/the-blue-books-reports/report-of-the-commissioners-of-inquiry-into-the-state-of-education-in-wales#?c=&m=&s=&cv=&xywh=-707%2C121%2C4652%2C3951, accessed July 9, 2021.

Roberts, J. (2002). The Latin Trade. In J. Barnard and D. F. McKenzie, eds., *The Cambridge History of the Book in Britain, Vol. IV: 1557–1695.* Cambridge: Cambridge University Press, pp. 141–73.

Roser, M. (2013). Books. *Our World in Data*, https://ourworldindata.org/books, accessed July 9, 2021.

Ross, D. n.d. Henry VIII's Act of Supremacy (1534) – original text. Britain Express, www.britainexpress.com/History/tudor/supremacy-henry-text.htm, accessed July 9, 2021.

Rummonds, R.-G. (2004). *Nineteenth-Century Printing Practices and the Iron Handpress.* London: The British Library.

Smith, W. (1874). *The Student's Gibbon: The History of the Decline and Fall of the Roman Empire, by Edward Gibbon, Abridged.* New York: Harper & Brothers.

Snell, M. (2019). Alfred the Great Quotations. *ThoughtCo*, www.thoughtco.com/alfred-the-great-quotes-1789330, accessed July 9, 2021.

St. Davids Cathedral's Famous Faces. *The History Press*, www.thehistorypress.co.uk/articles/st-davids-cathedral-s-famous-faces/, accessed July 9, 2021.

Thomas, D. (1991). *On the Air with Dylan Thomas: The Broadcasts.* Edited by Ralph Maud. New York: New Directions.

Thompson, E. P. (1963). *The Making of the English Working Class.* London: IICA.

Underwood, T. and Underwood, G. (1807). *The Repertory of Patent Inventions, and Other Discoveries and Improvements in Arts, Manufactures, and Agriculture.* London: J. Wyatt, Repertory Office.

Wales. (2015). Colophon Foundry, www.colophon-foundry.org/custom/wales/, accessed July 9, 2021.

Walters, H. (1998). The Periodical Press to 1914. In P. H. Jones and E. Rees, eds., *A Nation and Its Books: A History of the Book in Wales*. Aberystwyth: The National Library of Wales and the Aberystwyth Centre for the Book, pp. 197–208.

Welsh Journals. n.d. National Library of Wales, https://journals.library.wales/search?range%5Bmin%5D=1735&range%5Bmax%5D=2007&alt=*%3A*&page=1&refine=&alt=*%3A*&sort=score&order=desc&rows=12, accessed July 9, 2021.

Welsh Language Act. (1967). *Legislation.gov.uk*, www.legislation.gov.uk/ukpga/1967/66/enacted, accessed July 9, 2021.

Welsh Language Act. (1993). *Legislation.gov.uk*, www.legislation.gov.uk/ukpga/1993/38/contents, accessed July 9, 2021.

Whitteridge, G. (1973). The Identity of Sir Thomas Malory, Knight-Prisoner. *The Review of English Studies*, 24(95), pp. 257–65.

Williams, G. (1998). The Renaissance and Reformation. In P. H. Jones and E. Rees, eds., *A Nation and Its Books: A History of the Book in Wales*. Aberystwyth: The National Library of Wales and the Aberystwyth Centre for the Book, pp. 41–54.

Wood, M. n.d. William the Conqueror: A Thorough Revolutionary. *BBC History Trails*, www.bbc.co.uk/history/trail/conquest/norman/william_the_conqueror_02.shtml, accessed July 9, 2021.

Wright, T. (1863). Of the Character, Customs, and Habits of This People (the Irish): From *The Topography of Ireland* by Silvester Giraldus Cambrensis, 1187. Library Ireland, www.libraryireland.com/articles/CambrensisTopographyDistinction3-10/CambrensisTopographyDistinction3-10.html, accessed July 9, 2021.

Yr Amserau. n.d. Welsh Newspapers, National Library of Wales, https://newspapers.library.wales/browse/4239147, accessed July 9, 2021.

Cambridge Elements ☰

Publishing and Book Culture

SERIES EDITOR
Samantha Rayner
University College London

Samantha Rayner is Professor of Publishing and Book Cultures at UCL. She is also Director of UCL's Centre for Publishing, co-Director of the Bloomsbury CHAPTER (Communication History, Authorship, Publishing, Textual Editing and Reading) and co-Chair of the Bookselling Research Network.

ASSOCIATE EDITOR
Leah Tether
University of Bristol

Leah Tether is Professor of Medieval Literature and Publishing at the University of Bristol. With an academic background in medieval French and English literature and a professional background in trade publishing, Leah has combined her expertise and developed an international research profile in book and publishing history from manuscript to digital.

ABOUT THE SERIES

This series aims to fill the demand for easily accessible, quality texts available for teaching and research in the diverse and dynamic fields of Publishing and Book Culture. Rigorously researched and peer-reviewed Elements will be published under themes, or 'Gatherings'. These Elements should be the first check point for researchers or students working on that area of publishing and book trade history and practice: we hope that, situated so logically at Cambridge University Press, where academic publishing in the UK began, it will develop to create an unrivalled space where these histories and practices can be investigated and preserved.

Cambridge Elements $\equiv$

Publishing and Book Culture

Publishing and Book History

Gathering Editor: Andrew Nash

Andrew Nash is Reader in Book History and Director of the
London Rare Books School at the Institute of English Studies,
University of London. He has written books on Scottish and
Victorian Literature, and edited or co-edited numerous
volumes including, most recently, *The Cambridge History of the
Book in Britain, Volume 7* (CUP, 2019).

Gathering Editor: Leah Tether

Leah Tether is Professor of Medieval Literature and Publishing
at the University of Bristol. With an academic background in
medieval French and English literature and a professional
background in trade publishing, Leah has combined her
expertise and developed an international research profile in
book and publishing history from manuscript to digital.

ELEMENTS IN THE GATHERING

A full series listing is available at: www.cambridge.org/EPBC